A RABBI & A PREACHER GO TO A
PRIDE PARADE

Smyth & Helwys Publishing, Inc.
6316 Peake Road
Macon, Georgia 31210-3960
1-800-747-3016
©2019 by Bert Montgomery
All rights reserved.

Cover illustration by Greg Cravens

Library of Congress Cataloging-in-Publication Data

Names: Montgomery, Bert, author.
Title: A rabbi and a preacher go to a pride parade / by Bert Montgomery.
Description: Macon : Smyth & Helwys, 2019.
Identifiers: LCCN 2018040094 | ISBN 9781641730709 (pbk. : alk. paper)
Subjects: LCSH: Love--Religious aspects--Christianity. | Interpersonal
relations--Religious aspects--Christianity. | Homosexuality--Religious
aspects--Christianity.
Classification: LCC BV4639 .M5869 2019 | DDC 261.8/35766--dc23
LC record available at https://lccn.loc.gov/2018040094

This breezy, down-on-the-ground, readable book is made for personal perusal or Sunday school classes and other study groups who want stimulating pieces to get them going. Bert has that disarming way of opening up the LGBTQ+ issue and whacking you up against the head with some powerful biblical challenge you had not anticipated. What is unstated in the book is the kind of courage it takes to be Bert Montgomery in Mississippi and the integrity of witness he has now sustained there for a decade. Enjoy his humor but do not let it obscure the faithfulness and commitment he has embodied in his life and ministry.

—**Tex Sample**
Pastor, Trinity United Methodist Church
Kansas City, Missouri

Employing thoughtful intelligence, spasmic wit, and the Healer's wholistic approach to Scriptures, Pastor Bert Montgomery issues a clarion call to Christians the nation over to live out the "wildly inclusive love of Jesus." *A Rabbi & a Preacher Go to a Pride Parade* may sound like a joke, but Montgomery isn't fooling around when he notes that in most churches in America, the LGBTQ community is not welcome. Taking up the admonition that he is to be an advocate for those living in the margins, Pastor Bert boldly challenges his own community of Starkville, Mississippi, to model the love they wish to see in the world. When the residents of Starkville rise to the challenge, Pastor Bert is the least surprised of all. He knows the transformative love of Jesus can change the most bigoted of hearts. If it's inspiration and understanding you seek, read this book.

—**Karen Spears Zacharias**
Author of *Christian Bend: A Novel*

A Rabbi & a Preacher Go to a Pride Parade

and Other Musings, Sermons, and Such

Bert Montgomery

Also by Bert Montgomery

Elvis, Willie, Jesus & Me:
The Musings and Mutterings of a Church Misfit

Psychic Pancakes & Communion Pizza:
More Musings and Mutterings of a Church Misfit

Of Mice and Ministers:
Musings and Conversations about Life, Death, Grace, and Everything

Going Back to New Orleans:
Post-Katrina Reconnections and Recollections

This book is for
David Nowell and Renee Sappington—
two Mississippians
whose deep faith, love for Jesus, and outward Christian witness
continue to inspire me

and

for my many LGBTQ friends in Starkville, Mississippi,
and everywhere else,
because, to paraphrase the contemporary prophetic voice of
Stefani Joanne Angelina Germanotta,

you're beautiful in your way,
'cause God makes no mistakes,
you're on the right track,
Baby, you were born this way

Contents

Part 3: The *Sermons*

Part 4: The *And Such*

Foreword

The state of Mississippi has never been known as a bastion for equality or inclusion. This has certainly been true in regard to the African-American struggle for civil rights, but it has also been true for other minority groups, particularly the LGBTQ (lesbian, gay, bisexual, transgender, queer) community. Mississippi House Bill 1523, one of the most vicious and bigoted anti-LGBTQ laws in the country, currently grants broad permission to discriminate against LGBTQ individuals based on one's "free exercise of religious belief." Being denied public services and accommodations in your own hometown and state due to your sexuality or gender identity is oppressive and dehumanizing.

This exclusion is often most profound for LGBTQ individuals within faith communities. Fueled by homophobic and transphobic theologies, many religious leaders have condemned and excluded these individuals from places of worship. This deep and overwhelming alienation not only from faith communities but also from the belief that God loves them has caused lasting wounds to the souls of LGBTQ folk at the hands of "God's people."

Yet when all hope seems lost, God's love is found in the most unlikely places. Deep in the heart of the Magnolia State, as you leave the cotton fields of the flat and expansive delta and begin climbing into the eastern hills, you find the town of Starkville, home to Mississippi State University. You'd never suspect that this quaint little southern town had a Baptist preacher who was a pioneer and unrelenting public advocate of LGBTQ inclusion and equality. That individual is my dear friend and ally, the Rev. Bert Montgomery.

Bert's tireless work and dedication to welcoming and affirming LGBTQ folk into University Baptist Church and advocating for their equality at the city and state level is nothing less than the twenty-first-century manifestation of Jesus' gospel. In a climate of oppression and hate, Bert has courageously been the voice of love and inclusion to God's LGBTQ children in a state and denomination that largely denies their equality. He is one of the most sincere and genuine LGBTQ advocates we have in our struggle for equality and inclusion.

Like Dr. Martin Luther King Jr., Bert recognizes that what changes legislation, policy, and, most important, the human heart are our personal relationships with others. When someone gets to know you as a person who happens to be LGBTQ, it's much more difficult for them to cling to the "us and them" mentality that permeates our politics and faith communities. It's through love that radical change takes root and grows. With Bert's infectious humor and great storytelling ability, he bears witness to this truth in his new book, *A Rabbi & a Preacher Go to a Pride Parade.*

With a keen knowledge of Scripture and an unapologetic willingness to speak truth to power, Bert shares intimate personal encounters of spiritual transformation that have taken place throughout his ministry and public advocacy. From musings on the church's similarity to *Seinfeld*'s "Soup Nazi" to sermons that confront homophobia and call us to a greater love, Bert gives the reader an in-depth look into how his faith guides him in creating inclusivity not only within the Baptist church but also in the city of Starkville, the state of Mississippi, and beyond. I'm so honored to call him my friend and brother in Christ.

—*Rev. Maurice "Bojangles" Blanchard*
True Colors Ministry
Highland Baptist Church, Louisville, Kentucky

Part 1

The Context

Why This Book?

(A Prologue)

About the Book

Over the past decade or more, I have written and preached about Jesus *and* . . . life, death, suicide, depression, hope, politics, economics, sports, board games, curse words, racism, prejudice, immigration, Carrie Fisher, Janis Joplin, Arlo Guthrie, Martin Luther King, Jr., Thomas Merton, Advent, Christmas, Lent, Easter, actors, murderers, pizza, pancakes, baptism, Communion, giving blood, horror movies, TV shows, health care, the Allman Brothers, the Blues Brothers, the Statler Brothers, James Brown, Elvis Presley, Willie Nelson, Harry Potter, and Farrah Fawcett. There is even an entire book of Hurricane Katrina/New Orleans stories with my name on it. However, I am occasionally asked if "the gay issue" is the only thing I ever write and preach about. This book will do nothing to counter that perception, though, since it *is* one hundred percent about the so-called "gay issue." Oh, by the way, it is about *people*, and people are *not* "issues."

Inspired by the initial backlash from fellow Christians to a proposed first-ever Pride parade in Starkville, Mississippi (we'll get to that in a moment), I wrote a column about Jesus being a part of the parade, and how I, a preacher, and my friend, a rabbi, had also planned to be in it. At the same time, larger Christian organizations have been facing tumultuous internal conflicts centered on God, the Bible, and LGBTQ inclusion.[1] I had an idea, and I pitched it to my friends at Smyth & Helwys Publishing: let's assemble into one accessible volume all my

---

1. My own Cooperative Baptist Fellowship, which I dearly love, being among them.

LGBTQ-themed columns and sermons. And here you have it—the *gay* collection!

All of the "musings" have previously appeared as columns in newspapers such as the *Starkville Daily News* and the *Clarion Ledger* and/or at various online sites including Huffington Post, Baptist News Global, Red Letter Christians, and the Cooperative Baptist Fellowship's Patheos blog. A few of them have already appeared in the other musings books, in which case those titles are identified. As far as the sermons and such, each one contains a brief note of introduction and context.

Let me briefly address what this book is *not*. It is not my concern here to construct some sort of systematic queer theology. Nor do I attempt to specifically examine, explain, or reinterpret the handful of "clobber passages"—those five or six specific verses most often used to justify spiritual, emotional, psychological, and even physical attacks on LGBTQ people. There are many excellent resources already available that do those things far better than I ever could. I have included at the end of this book a short list of references that might satisfy your curiosity or at least give you a good start in your investigation.

Instead, every piece in this collection arises from relationships: relationships with Jesus and relationships with others. Each reflection is born from personal encounters with the Holy Spirit moving in and through people I know, respect, trust, and love. The theology here is simple: (1) the Holy Spirit is wild, reckless, and uncontrollable; (2) each and every person bears the image of God; (3) Jesus comes to us over and over again in the people in whom we might least expect; and, (4) above everything else, we are to love God, love ourselves, and love others, and then treat others the way we would want others to treat us if we were in their shoes. These simple, biblical themes flow continuously through this book as I share reflections and stories from my experiences as a Christian minister surrounded by friends who identify as LGBTQ.

A final word about this book: It covers a fourteen-year span, from the oldest musing to the most recent reflection. The pieces are not organized in chronological order although I often note the date and specific context of each piece to serve as time markers. As I previewed the assembled manuscript—independent essays patched together like a quilt—I noticed how, over the passing of time, my faith deepened, my theology evolved, and my conviction grew stronger. I invite you as you read to pause before each entry and to pay attention to the markers as we move together from one setting to another, and as we traverse more than a decade in a short time. I pray that the scenery you take in along this trail will encourage, challenge, and resonate with you as you continue your own walk with Christ.

About the Parade

It was kind of like a great Donovan song: first there was a Pride parade, then was no Pride parade, then there was.[2]

A young couple in our community and in our church, Bailey and Emily, felt it was long past time for Starkville to have a Pride parade. They submitted all the paperwork and jumped through all the bureaucratic hoops the city government required; everything appeared set to go. There was the mere formality of official approval, but, like other special-event requests over the past several years, the Pride parade was on the Board of Aldermen's consent agenda to move forward without objection.

Word began to spread among some Christian leaders that gay folks would be flocking to Starkville, dancing naked in our streets (and who knows what else), and that we would quickly become known as a "sin city." Aldermen were contacted. On short notice, the event was removed from the consent agenda and brought out for public discussion and a vote. At the February 20, 2018, meeting of the Board of Aldermen, several citizens spoke in favor of having the parade; a few spoke against it. Starkville has seven aldermen. The vote was 4-3 against having the Pride parade. The LGBTQ community and their friends, colleagues, and family members were highly disillusioned with the town where they had previously felt welcomed and respected.

Immediate national attention turned to "Mississippi's College Town." Renowned LGBTQ-equality attorney Roberta Kaplan filed a discrimination lawsuit against the City of Starkville on behalf of the Starkville Pride organization. The reality of a certain loss in court and

---

2. If you don't know the Donovan song "First There Is a Mountain," or even Donovan for that matter, do an internet search. Better yet, ask an old hippie.

its significant financial consequences for the city, along with all the negative national coverage, led the aldermen to revisit the matter.

At the board's meeting on March 6, one of the four original "nay"-voting aldermen abstained, leaving a 3-3 tie. In the case of tie votes, Starkville's mayor can cast a tie-breaking vote; Mayor Lynn Spruill, then, cast her vote in favor of the parade.

The parade went off on March 24 without a hitch! Everyone had a lot of fun, and it had by far the largest crowd for a single event in Starkville's history.[3]

So . . . there you have it. Not everything in this collection relates directly to Starkville's Pride parade; actually, most of it does not. If I learned anything from the entire Pride parade timeline, reactions, and the event itself, it is that some fourteen years after first "coming out" in a sermon as a welcoming and affirming Baptist preacher, and fourteen years of occasional columns and sermons about the church and LGBTQ inclusion, I probably have not written or preached about it nearly enough.

---

3. Other than events on Mississippi State's campus, of course.

The Parade:
A Summary of the Day

"The Good Lord had a hand in the whole event—and the parade—and I am so thankful," Janean Romines said a few days afterward. Janean, a member of University Baptist Church, was involved in the behind-the-scenes work leading up to Starkville's Pride events, so she was in a good spot to see God's hand moving through it all.

It was a beautiful spring morning that Saturday, March 24. Starkville Pride's day of events began with a Queer Art Market in a small park on the edge of downtown. Local artists and vendors—gay and straight—had gathered to sell everything from handmade jewelry to pottery to paintings to gourmet popcorn and baked goods.

UBC had our church display set up, and church members were passing out stickers. One sticker design had a rainbow on it with the message, "U-B-U at UBC"; the other design read, "UBC: the church your mother warned you about." I had a table next to the church's to peddle my own wares.[1]

Rumor had it that the infamous Westboro Baptist folks had threatened to come from Kansas, but they were nowhere to be found. Other similar loud, angry people did show up, though. They held large signs, spewed hellfire and brimstone through bullhorns, and stood directly across the street from the market area, hurling verbal assaults at people as they parked and walked to the market area.

---

1. "To peddle my wares" is a phrase, which, as used here, means "to sell my books."

Another group showed up and served as an interesting buffer between the market and the wielders of God's wrath—a local church that practices "gay conversion therapy." These were men and women who believe God delivered them from being gay. They did not judge the LGBTQ community, but were kind-hearted and pleasant. The pastor of this group even moved between one of the bigger, louder men and some individuals who were the target of his screaming rage. The pastor gently, gracefully, stood face to face with the man to divert the wrath toward himself so that others would not be harassed.

Then, we lined up for the parade.

UBCers Bailey, Emily, and Alex were at the front carrying the Starkville Pride banner. There was a small drumline led by local musicians (including UBCers Joe and Jimmy) playing various percussion instruments, singing songs, and spreading joy. UBC member Derek printed a large rainbow banner that declared "U-B-U AT UBC: Come Celebrate God's Wildly Inclusive Love."

The rabbi, Seth Oppenheimer, along with a few other members of his congregation, walked with the UBC group. Seth carried a sign with a message from the Torah, written in Hebrew, reminding us of God's instruction to love others as we love ourselves. I grabbed an available sign that warned, "Be careful who you hate; one day it might be someone you love."

Children were everywhere, dancing, laughing, clapping; older folks were doing the same. Drag queens danced and waved and paused for pictures. All races, all ages, all genders, all economic classes, all nationalities, all political allegiances and all variety of religious beliefs (or lack thereof)—everybody came together to celebrate diversity and inclusion.

In the days leading up to the parade, a few members of our congregation had expressed concern that there may be violence toward the participants, or, specifically, toward our church group. After the parade, I learned that the worry was shared by several others in the church, too. Emily and Bailey and other organizers had received hostile, hate-filled messages and emails prior to the weekend's events. Yet, apart from the small group of angry, screaming protesters, from start to finish it was a remarkably joy-filled celebration of the wide diversity of God's beautiful kingdom. The good Lord's hand was in the whole event, indeed!

Pride, through the Eyes of University Baptist Church

I invited several of the UBC folks who participated in the Pride parade to share their own stories: what the parade meant to them, favorite moments, how the parade was an expression of their faith, and why they felt UBC's visibility was important. Rabbi Seth Oppenheimer (who, along with a couple of others from his congregation, marched with our UBC group in the parade) also contributed to the conversation.

What did the Pride parade mean to you?

Bailey M.: The parade was the culmination of four years of fighting for a seat at the table when it comes to LGBTQ inclusion in Starkville. I've spent the entirety of my time in Starkville being an advocate for my community and trying to make the city, the university, and the community listen to us. When our application was denied, people came out of the woodwork to support and encourage us. I was shocked by how many people were willing to put their name on the line and stand up for us and Starkville Pride.

Emily T.: For me, Starkville Pride was the culmination of a long personal journey. As a closeted gay kid at Starkville High, I never could have imagined marching down main street Starkville with my girlfriend at the front of a Pride parade. I am extremely proud of Starkville for coming together and making the parade happen; the support we received (after the parade permit was denied) only confirmed to me that Starkville is a lot more accepting than I thought when I was in high school. People I never would have thought were allies came up to me after the parade and told me they were so proud of me.

Melissa G.: The pushback showed us we still have a lot of work to do, but the level of community support showed us that we've made huge strides of progress.

Rachel F.: Starkville's Pride parade was very significant to me as an established community member in the area. It was very moving to see a community come together and advocate for something that a large proportion of the community wanted to see take place. This parade reminded me that if what seems like a small portion of a community works hard at something, and puts ongoing effort into something, it can indeed be achieved.

Diana O.: It meant that the voices of the young and the marginalized were strong enough to drown out the establishment. Progress!

Susie U.: Starkville's Pride absolutely amazed me. I could not believe that this itty-bitty town had that much love and support for me and my LGBTQ family. It was the first time in my life that I've ever been out and proud in the town where I lived, and I felt nothing but love the entire time.

Rabbi Seth O.: Being able to be fully public and seen supporting members of the nontraditional gender [communities] and non-traditional orientation communities was extremely important to me. These folks are my friends, colleagues, and students. They need to know that I view them as exactly that—my friends, colleagues, and students. Nothing more and nothing less. They are deserving of human dignity and rights.

Linda B.: As a native of Starkville and heterosexual from a very conservative family, joining in a Pride parade celebration was not on my radar. The experienced stretched me spiritually and revealed sides of the faith community that were unknown to me.

Pam S.: I had first thought I would be a parade observer, but I quickly realized that I had to participate because of those I care about, however small the gesture might seem. The parade would have been just as powerful without me, but I would not have been nearly so affected. I was 71 at the time and this was my first march (the number of major marches during my lifetime makes this an embarrassing confession). Experiencing the joy and camaraderie among the participants and the vast majority of the observers was meaningful to me.

Joe E.: The Pride parade was a joyful exhalation of the pent-up frustrations and challenges of an entire community. It was a coming out party in every sense of the term. It was a group of people who have always been here acknowledging and being acknowledged.

Derek W.: I never pictured myself marching in a Pride parade. When my community tried to deny my right to march, I knew I had to stand up against such hate and march on with my head held high. Living in the shadows and closets is no life compared to that sunny day and what I finally believed in my heart—that I was never broken, cursed, or had cause to be ashamed. I had reason to celebrate!

Chartese J.: Understanding the importance of inclusiveness is vital. The Pride parade showed that not only do we have a voice in the community but we also are able to show love and its ability to overcome our differences. To see the number of people who came out to support was overwhelming. Being able to make the local news was very impressive.

Daniel P.: Starkville's Pride parade meant I could be myself completely, and that things were going to be OK. I felt safe, like I could let my guard down. It was a day of absolute unconditional love!

Ashley B.: Starkville Pride meant hope. It meant that even after the struggle to get it approved, there is still hope that the community that I choose to live in will love and accept me. It meant that the students I mentor can have a safe place to come out and be themselves without fear. It meant hope.

What was your favorite aspect of the Pride parade?

Teagan W.: My favorite part of the parade was seeing people I didn't realize would be there. It was like an unspoken acknowledgment that there are people I know outside of UBC that are accepting of the LGBTQ+ community like I am. Also, I loved being able to help carry the UBC banner for part of the parade!

Pam S.: There were no sermons or speeches (albeit some yelling from one tiny corner) but lots of positive interaction. People smiled and waved, many coming out of stores and restaurants to join in. Participants ran to observers (and vice versa) to exchange hugs. And within it all there was quiet, if you wanted it, to think your own thoughts about what was happening.

Ashley B.: I was able to be one of the few people carrying the piece of the Section 93 Pride Flag[1] at the end of the parade. Though we had several protestors following us, as we walked more and more people started walking with us and stood between us and the protestors, forcing them back farther and farther from the parade itself.

Daniel P.: I remember at one point looking behind me and seeing this huge wave of people just everywhere! It was truly breathtaking! I also loved randomly running into friends I had a history with since I was a kid. It was nothing like the pride parades I had been part of in Atlanta. This felt historic yet extremely personal at the same time.

Diana O.: My 8-year old daughter (Arya) waved her equality flag the whole time and helped our friend Susie (who just happens to be gay) to push the stroller of her disabled son for most of the parade. Keep in mind that my daughter has disabilities of her own but it was more

---

1. "Section 93" is a rainbow flag, 25 feet long, 14 feet wide, that has traveled around the country and will hang in the Smithsonian. For more information about its journey to Starkville, see Logan Kirkland, "Historic LGBT flag makes its way to Starkville," *Starkville Daily News*, 13 March 2018, <starkvilledailynews.com/content/historic-lgbt-flag-makes-its-way-starkville> (accessed 7 January 2019).

important to her to help someone that she loves (Miss Susie) than the fact that she was tired.

Susie U.: My most favorite memory was watching Arya help push Jonathan's wheelchair the entire parade route. That route had to have been difficult for her as long as it was and with her limitations, but she lasted the whole time. It reminded me of how much stronger we are when we are working together and when we are helping others.

Rachel F.: There is a particular moment during the pride parade that I will never forget. I had the opportunity to be one of the individuals that carried the historic rainbow flag at the very end of the parade. There was a surreal moment that occurred before the parade began in which I looked around and noticed the many different types of individuals that were there holding the flag with me. There were no questions or requirements that had to be achieved in order to be qualified to hold the flag throughout the parade and, to me, that was a great representation of what the entire Pride parade was symbolizing.

Pam S.: I did not expect the huge number of people or the degree of acceptance and community and just happiness; it was both mesmerizing and unforgettable. The ease and openness, the flags and signs, the music and dancing, the sea of bright color combined to create not a militant march but a celebration of life and relationship.

Melissa G.: To me the best part about pride was the energy and seeing how incredibly happy everyone was to be open about who they are. Aside from the protestors, everyone I met was smiling and just happy to be out showing their support.

Linda B.: Because I have been active in an evangelical church all my life, this was the first time someone loudly informed me that I did not know God. On the other side of the community, the love and relief from the acceptance among my LGBTQ friends was palpable.

Derek W.: There were angry protesters preaching hellfire and damnation. They were at most an annoyance though. I loved how I could march with my church family, my pastor, a rabbi, and my God knowing love conquers hate. I especially admired people like Linda and many others through the day being allies to the LGBTQ community and blocking, distracting, or returning Bible verses—preaching love and understanding back to them.

Joe E.: The whole experience of getting to play and sing in the (marching percussion) band was fantastic. It was a pure expression of joy and community.

Emily T.: The parade was the first time that Bailey's parents and my parents had ever met, and that was a special moment. It was also important to me that my parents marched in the parade with UBC. They have never been that public in supporting who I am, and to see them wearing ally buttons and marching alongside my church family was really special. My mom keeps her ally button from the parade on her desk at home, and every time I see it I remember that moment.

Bailey M.: My favorite moment from the parade was when my parents and Emily's parents met for the first time. We first met up with Em's parents and they quickly asked where they could fall in line to march in the parade. My mom and step-dad marched behind us. When we finished the route, my parents were standing with us when her parents walked up (wearing ally buttons, by the way), and everyone started talking about how glad they were we had met. It was amazing to feel the support of both of our families and have that day and event be the first time they had all met. The parade was one of the most amazing experiences in my life because I was standing with almost 3,000 people telling the city, the state, and the country LGBTQ people are welcome in Starkville and we are here to celebrate and support the community no matter what.

Rachel F: When those of us holding the (Section 93) flag made the turn on to Main Street of downtown Starkville, there was almost an overwhelming sense of joy. As we looked down the entire parade route that occurred on Main Street itself, you could see several hundred individuals standing on the sidelines of the parade cheering, dancing, celebrating, and some even dressed in pride attire. This moment was touching because it was then that we realized the few hundred people we were expecting had turned into a few thousand. This moment will remain the most memorable moment of the parade for me, as in that moment, I realized that the hard work and efforts had paid off, that people really do care despite our differences, and an entire community can come together and stand up for each other.

Ashley B.: There was one group of African-American ladies. . . . I remember three in particular, but I believe there were five or six of them, sitting around the open tailgate of an older SUV. They were waving their flags and jumping up and down, cheering and clapping, and one sweet woman in particular was yelling "Those are my babies! Look at my babies!" And, I lost it. I cried, and I'm crying now as I type this. That was my happiest moment of the entire Pride weekend, and I wish I knew who she was so I could hug her.

Pam S.: My favorite moments were seeing the joy (amid emotional exhaustion) of individuals who planned and organized this day, survived the approval process, and were thriving in the moment and the resultant reality. "Success" is far too shallow a description.

Daniel P.: I had a very difficult year leading up to this event and had been questioning why I had decided to come back to Mississippi. The loving supportive LGBTQ community I once was a part of wasn't part of my daily life any more, and I had a very hard time trying to create a new one here. The day gave me hope, though. I knew when I met so many beautiful people that told me their stories and how I, personally, inspired them just by being myself that perhaps I was here for a reason.

How was the parade an expression of your faith? Why was it important for UBC to be a visible part of the parade?

Rabbi Seth O.: People who feel they are outsiders often believe they are closed off from traditional religious communities. I wanted to be loud and clear by walking in Kippah and Tallit and carrying a Torah line in Hebrew that the Jewish community of the Golden Triangle welcomes all people of all orientations and identifications as full and important members.

Joe E.: My attendance at the parade was an expression of my faith in that I was expressing my love for a community that is so often ridiculed, rejected, and scorned by our society at large.

Chartese J.: For my church to be part of the Pride parade and all the festivities tells enough.

Melissa G.: It was nice to see different representatives from local churches at pride. So many LGBT people's perception of Christianity is the protestors that were yelling at us, but the reality is that there are many faith communities where LGBT individuals are welcomed with open arms.

Derek W.: While I believe "pride" is a sin, I know in my heart "Pride" festivals are in obedience and glory to God. To know God tells us to come out into the light. We are not boastful nor thinking we're more or better than anyone else. "Pride" is our chance to admire we are just as we were made, your neighbors. "Pride" celebrates being lifted back up and walking hand in hand. "Pride" celebrates my God and reminds me God gave us the rainbow as a promise the sun will come out again no matter how bad the storms in life may be. Rejoice in the light and you'll never suffer in shadows or closets again.

Teagan W.: Starkville's Pride parade meant being able to share the inclusive love that I have found at UBC. I was so excited to show everyone at the parade how cool and awesome our church is and that we want them to visit and join us in discovering the affirming and loving spirit we know. I was at our table for a short time and speaking to people stopping by, and it was amazing to see the looks on their faces to know there is a welcoming place they can come and share their thoughts and feelings about God/Jesus/Spirituality/Higher Powers. I love UBC and that made it easy to share about our wildly inclusive community.

Diana O.: The fact that UBC was so prominent renewed my own faith in this community and is one of the main reasons that I began attending services at UBC.

Susie U.: Although I hadn't darkened the doorstep of UBC at the time, it was very important to me that it was so visible because it allowed me to see what UBC's mission was and that they truly believed in and would stand up for that mission, as evidenced by their overwhelming support and presence in the weekend. Which eventually led me to visiting and finding a whole new world of friends at a time when I needed it the most.

Bailey M.: I've found a family in UBC that I never thought I would find in a church. To see everyone I love and care for standing beside me in one of the toughest fights I have been through has been one of the most humbling and encouraging experiences. Having the church not only support the parade but march in full-on pride spirit was amazing. To know a community of faith is available to those who are religious in the community is very comforting and I am grateful to UBC for being that community.

Emily T.: The parade was important as an expression of my faith because, as a gay kid (a closeted gay kid), I never felt welcome in the church. I never understood why the church would hate a people for who they loved. That feeling, knowing the church I grew up in and loved thought who I was an abomination, was something I did not want other kids to feel. UBC's marching in the parade means that kids know there is a church family in Starkville that will love them for who they are, not just tolerate them. UBC's marching in the parade shows the true love of God, and I am extremely proud to be a part of a congregation that shows what the body of Christ should look like.

Rachel F.: I began going to church in middle school on my own consistently. I served in leadership roles, went on three out-of-country "mission trips," and was a student leader each year of high school. Much of my impression of church/religion/spirituality changed once I came out, and in return, I felt rejection from those who had helped "bring me up" in the church family that I very much identified with. I began to feel as though somehow the work I had done in the church until that point was null and void now that I was coming out as my true self, which happened to contradict what my church family believed in. Having UBC there at the Pride events showed our community that there are churches around Starkville that are accepting and welcoming. Not only did having UBC present at those events remind individuals like me that there are great, open places, it reminded me that there is a place of religion that will value the work I have done for others and also recognize, and be OK, that I am also a part of the LGBTQ community. It was incredibly important for UBC to be there and be visible at the events. I even heard several say, "That's a *church!* Look, there is even a *church* walking in the parade!"

Ashley B.: The first thing you hear in the South from anyone struggling with their sexuality is, "but I'm a Christian"; the same goes for the first argument anyone brings up to someone coming out, "but I thought you were a Christian." I am not sure where we, as a society, have come to believe you have to be one or the other, gay or a Christian, but you do not have to choose. For that reason, the parade was important to my expression of faith, and I am glad UBC is so visible, always (not only during the parade). Now, if we can just get parents on board with not making this their first argument.

Pam S.: Maybe these words from Hebrews 13 (The Message) describe the Pride parade best: "Make sure you don't take things for granted and go slack in working for the common good; share what you have with others. God takes particular pleasure in acts of worship—a different kind of 'sacrifice'—that take place in kitchen and workplace and on the streets."

Part 2

The *Musings*

A Rabbi, a Preacher, and Jesus

(Or, People You Might See at a Pride Parade)

This column was written a few days following the original Starkville Board of Aldermen meeting in which the aldermen voted to deny the parade permit.[1] It ran in the Starkville Daily News, *the* Clarion-Ledger *(Jackson, Mississippi—in print and online), and online via Baptist News Global.*

A rabbi and a preacher go to a Pride parade . . .

That is as far as I have gotten at this point, because while everybody loves a parade, it seems that four Starkville, Mississippi, aldermen do not; they blocked me from getting to the punch line. My friend Seth Oppenheimer, a rabbi, and I planned to be a part of Starkville's proposed first-ever Pride parade.

I love parades. I grew up in and around New Orleans. Every spring there are numerous parades—multiple parades every day for several weeks—leading up to Mardi Gras Day. And Mardi Gras Day, also called Fat Tuesday, is a day filled with (you guessed it) even *more* parades. In New Orleans, they look for reasons to parade in the streets. Grandma died? Get on down to the French Quarter and we'll send her off with a parade!

I have not lived in the Crescent City for thirty years, yet I am still not accustomed to the noticeable lack of parades everywhere else I have lived. There is always a Christmas parade, of course, and maybe a homecoming parade, and in Starkville there is the getting-ready-for-

---

1. I refer you back to the book's prologue for a brief summary and timeline related to the Board of Aldermen and their denial-then-approval of Starkville, Mississippi's first-ever, and absolutely fabulous, Pride parade.

baseball-season Dudy Gras parade.[2] But I think we would all be so much healthier and happier if we just had more parades.

I am confused, then, as to why four of Starkville's aldermen said "nay" to having another parade. They did not give a reason for their vote, but exited quickly out the back door when the meeting ended.

Perhaps they feel that two parades for a town our size is one, or even two, too many. A third might force us to change our nickname from "StarkVegas" to "StarkOrleans," and that just doesn't have the same "ring" to it.

I sense, though, that there is something more troubling at work here. Something unpleasant, something wrong, something discriminatory.

It appears that the four naysaying aldermen do not like gay folks. Their vote suggests that LGBTQ people do not belong in Starkville. This is not the first time; we have been through this before. Just a few years ago we had tense board meetings regarding a nondiscriminatory policy protecting the rights of LGBTQ individuals employed by the city, and more tense board meetings about the city's "plus-one" insurance benefits offerings. The Pride parade vote echoes those votes in targeting a particular group of people and saying, "We do not want you here."

The most disappointing aspect of their vote is the apparent "Christian" reasoning behind it: that God, also, doesn't like gays.

Such an understanding of God is too small. Interpreting the Holy Scriptures in order to condemn the LGBTQ community is too narrow, too legalistic, too short-sighted. A limited view of God and Scripture fails to see the larger story of scandalous grace at work from Genesis through Revelation; it fails to follow the unpredictable Spirit of God moving freely, without restraint, and always finding the most excluded "outsiders" to welcome them in; and it fails to be humbled by the gospel texts that reveal the wildly inclusive love of Jesus and the wide diversity of God's kingdom.

---

2. For those not familiar with baseball at Mississippi State University, "Dudy Gras" is a popular event that kicks off the MSU baseball season (and falls during Mardi Gras season). There is an actual parade that moves through downtown Starkville and ends on campus at Dudy Noble Field, the home of Bulldog baseball.

Christians are involved in the Pride events. This I know, because the organizers, Bailey and Emily, are a part of my church family, and because several members of my church planned to participate.

Of course, some of those who would participate in the Pride parade are Buddhists. Some are Jewish. Some are atheists, agnostics, or are otherwise nonreligious. Yet committed Catholics, Episcopalians, Methodists, Presbyterians, Baptists, and so on would have been involved, too.

LGBTQ people work in our stores and in our schools. They cook or serve in our favorite restaurants. They do incredible, groundbreaking research, teach in the classrooms, and work behind the scenes as administrators and staff all over Mississippi State University's campus. They entertain us in school bands and drama clubs, and they excite us in sporting competitions. Like it or not, gay and transgender sisters and brothers sit in our church pews every Sunday—whether openly at the few gay-friendly churches or "in the closet" among the many not-so-gay-friendly churches.

It is a disgrace that the aldermen consider them second-class citizens. It is a disgrace that they do so while apparently believing prohibiting a parade is the "Christian" thing to do.

Every time in the Gospels that "God's men" (and they were all men) exclude, ignore, and marginalize or outright condemn categories of people, Jesus immediately turns up walking among, hanging out with, laughing and crying and eating with those "wrong kinds" of people. The scholars and teachers of God's Law were upset that Jesus would walk away from them; they accused Jesus of being a gluttonous drunkard and an immoral man.[3] Jesus preferred the company of wild sinners to the company of the good, "righteous" people.

It does not take much to imagine the religious leaders accusing Jesus of being gay, because, if we believe the Gospels, clearly Jesus would be laughing and celebrating with his friends at a Pride parade.

---

3. His public associations with women, including some with "questionable" reputations, caused Jesus' own sexual ethics to be in question (see Matt 11:19 and Luke 7:34).

I hope I will get the opportunity to join Jesus, my friend Rabbi Seth, and all my other friends and neighbors and church members as we walk together in Starkville's first-ever Pride parade in March.

Gays, Baptists, and Killer Tomatoes

My friend Michael and I have a lot in common.[1] We were both born and raised as Southern Baptists in the deep South. We both applaud the brilliant absurdity of the film *Attack of the Killer Tomatoes*. And we're both gay. Well, most of the time. I'm often frustrated, sad, or just flat tired. But when I'm not one of those things, I tend to be gay. Michael, no matter how he's feeling, is just always gay.

I was confused, then, when I heard that a prominent Southern Baptist seminary president may have suggested that babies might be born gay, and if they are, we Christians may have the responsibility to tinker about in the womb to ensure that they will *not* be gay.[2]

Now why would any Christian not want another person to be gay? If we are receiving the full and abundant life Christ offers us, I'd think we'd all be gay and enthusiastic from time to time.

My wife says I'm missing the point. Apparently, the word "gay" has changed. So I looked it up in Webster's Dictionary. There are the usual definitions such as "happily excited," "keenly alive and exuberant: having or inducing high spirits," and "bright, lively."

But then, sure enough, there is a fourth: "Homosexual; of, relating to, or used by homosexuals."

---

1. This musing is borrowed from *Elvis, Willie, Jesus & Me* (Macon: Smyth & Helwys, 2008).

2. "Is Your Baby Gay? What If You Could Know? What If You Could Do Something about It?" blog post by R. Albert Mohler Jr., 2 March 2007, <albert-mohler.com/2007/03/02/is-your-baby-gay-what-if-you-could-know-what-if-you-could-do-something-about-it-2/> (accessed 21 January 2019).

My wife went on to explain that this is why I am sometimes gay and sometimes not, but why Michael simply *is* gay. "Same word, different meanings," she said.

Oh.

So, thanks to my wife, I now understand that Dr. Albert Mohler, president of the Southern Baptist Theological Seminary, is not saying that the genes causing exuberance should be altered in fetuses but that the genes that may lead to homosexual behavior should be altered.

I'm still confused, though. Here's why: I've known Michael and his family since I was a kid. He has been and still is an active leader and teacher in church. Yep, Michael is gay (by the fourth definition), yet I still know him to be a man of deep and sincere faith. And because I know Michael, I cannot imagine going back in time to alter his genetic makeup in order to make him some sort of super-über-Christian. Hey—I've watched *Frankenstein* enough to be scared to death of trying to play God with creation.

Dr. Mohler presents ten points to consider should the time come in which parents can opt in or out of certain biological traits, including homosexuality. He emphasizes that "Christians who are committed to think in genuinely Christian terms should think carefully about these points." "These points" include the acknowledgment that no biological basis for homosexuality has yet been found—but if such a basis *were* discovered and could be reversed with, say, a hormone patch, Dr. Mohler "would support its use" (see his point #8 in the article).

I find it odd that Jesus is never mentioned in these important points that "Christians who are committed to think in genuinely Christian terms" should ponder. Maybe I'm not as "committed to think in genuinely Christian terms" as I had hoped, but I don't understand why Dr. Mohler fails to refer to Jesus. I went to the Gospels to do more research and—lo and behold!—Jesus has absolutely nothing to say about homosexuality.

Jesus does, however, have an awful lot to say about high-and-mighty religious experts speaking on behalf of God about who is "good" enough and who is not-quite or nowhere-near "good" enough for God. God's self-appointed "spokesmen" in the Gospels are the very ones who, in protecting their religious power and traditions, despise Jesus and lead the charge to crucify him.[3]

According to the Gospel accounts, Jesus has no time for petty religious games, and he prefers love over law and grace over judgment (though he sure comes down hard on the religious experts!). One of the preeminent teachings of Baptists is that Jesus is the ultimate revelation of God to humanity; therefore, all of Scripture is to be interpreted through the life, death, resurrection, and teachings of our Lord. This, then, leads me to believe that Jesus is more likely to be hanging out with Michael and his friends than sitting around in a room full of Bible experts discussing the top-ten proper "Christian" ways to think.

The next time I watch *Attack of the Killer Tomatoes* in my gay enthusiasm (by the first few definitions), I'll think of my gay friend Michael (by all the definitions, including the fourth) and wonder if he is sharing a laugh with Jesus as they watch one of our favorite movies together.

---

3. Yes, it's usually been men claiming to speak for God.

Of Pea Pods and Hurricanes

(Ode to Ellen DeGeneres, and Renee and Connie)

The following musing was composed in September 2005 while I was a student at the Baptist Seminary of Kentucky.[1] It was based on a news report that Pat Robertson publicly declared that Hurricane Katrina was God's judgment upon New Orleans because Ellen DeGeneres is gay. That news report was quickly pulled (but not until after I wrote my thoughts) when it was discovered to be a piece of satire not based on fact. However, as even snopes.com acknowledges, one didn't require much (if any) exaggeration to suggest that Pat Robertson would say such a thing. Brother Pat is fond of publicly pronouncing God's judgment in the aftermath of disasters and tragedies.[2]

In June 2009, my old Mississippi College friend Renee and her wife, Connie, spoke briefly at the Annual United Methodist Conference in Mississippi. They spoke of a particular congregation that has welcomed them, loved them, and helped nurture them in their faith. Understandably, their testimony created a bit of a stir. While I support dialogue and civil disagreement, and, technically, I "don't have a dog in this fight" (I'm a Baptist minister, not a Methodist one), I will not remain quiet while some openly question the integrity and the faith of a friend.

---

1. This musing was also included in *Psychic Pancakes & Communion Pizza* (Macon: Smyth & Helwys, 2011).

2. See David Mikkelson, "God's Wrath," 12 September 2005 (updated) <www.snopes.com/fact-check/gods-wrath/>; see also Frank James, "Pat Robertson Blames Haitian Devil Pact for Earthquake," NPR, 13 January 2010 <www.npr.org/sections/thetwo-way/2010/01/pat_robertson_blames_haitian_d.html>; and Michael Horton, "Yes, Pat Robertson blamed the Vegas shooting on 'disrespect' for Trump and the national anthem," *Washington Post*, 3 October 2017 <www.washingtonpost.com/news/acts-of-faith/wp/2017/10/03/yes-pat-robertson-blamed-the-vegas-shooting-on-disrespect-for-trump-and-the-national-anthem/?utm_term=.f0dda40eea80>.

So, acknowledging that the basis of this musing is actually fictional, I maintain that the spirit of this piece and the message I intended to convey are relevant and truthful.

Now then, Renee—how about we grab a cup of coffee sometime?

The Rev. Pat Robertson and I have a lot in common. We both hail from and still live in the South; I'm from Louisiana and now live in Kentucky, and Pat's from and still lives in Virginia.

We both value higher education. I love classrooms so much that I'm working on a second master's degree; heck, Pat values education so much that he *owns* an institution of higher learning. I live in a state where people race valuable horses; Pat breeds valuable racehorses. And, as if all of that weren't enough, Pat Robertson and I are both ordained Baptist ministers. Yep, me and Pat, Pat and me: like two peas from the same pod.

It just so happens that I also have a lot in common with Ellen DeGeneres. Ellen enjoys having her own television shows; I enjoy watching Ellen's television shows. Ellen's brother, Vance DeGeneres, used to be in a rock band called The Cold; I once saw Ellen's brother, Vance, play with his rock band The Cold. And, as if TV and rock 'n' roll weren't enough, Ellen DeGeneres and I were both born and raised in the New Orleans area. Yep, me and Ellen, Ellen and me: just like two peas from the same pod.

But then that would make Pat and Ellen from the same pod, too, wouldn't it?

I read somewhere that Pat blamed Ellen for Hurricane Katrina (say it ain't so, Pat!). Hmmmm . . . I guess it's a stretch to think that Ellen and Pat share a pea pod.

I wish I could help these peas get together. I wish I could get Ellen to . . . convince Ellen to . . . well, Ellen's not really at fault here as far as I can tell.

So I have to address Pat. I'm worried about us, Pat—two Baptist preachers from the Southland. I'm worried because I read the Gospels, and it is clear that Jesus saves his judgment for the religious leaders, the good, upstanding, righteous folks who feel that they are too "good" to love others, too "good" to serve others, too "good" to be friends with others. Jesus saves his words of judgment for those religious folks who are so "good" that they freely pass judgment on others who aren't "good enough."

It's really quite simple, Pat: Jesus has a whole lot to say about money, power, arrogance, and self-righteousness, but, doggone that Savior of ours, he never says one blasted word about sexual preferences. Not one! Go look it up for yourself.

Yes, I've got hang-ups and concerns—we all do. But Pat, I've got to take all of this into serious consideration, because, after all, I'm called to be like Jesus. And Jesus spends more time hanging out with, having fun with, living among, and loving the real people in the world—people who are not "good enough" by religious leaders' standards—than he does with religious leaders who have high opinions of themselves. And don't ever forget, Pat, it's religious leaders like us who led the charge to execute our Lord.

Pat, all I'm going by are your public statements, but your declarations seem to me to be pretentious, arrogant, and self-righteous. Besides, Pat, with all that wealth you've accumulated from your television station, your TV ministry, your books, and your horses—and let's not forget your fascination with political power—well, it's easy to imagine Jesus having a few choice words for you as he walks off to enjoy a cup of coffee with Ellen.

Pat, I love you, my brother, my pea-pod-sharing friend, but I'm choosing to follow Jesus on this one. If I hurry, I might be able to catch up with him and Ellen. I sure hope they have some chicory coffee at that coffee shop . . .

When Did *Seinfeld*'s "Soup Nazi" Become Our Model of Christian Conduct?

This column was written in May 2016 after the State of Mississippi passed HB-1523—the religious-objection law legalizing discrimination against LGBTQ people.

TV's *Seinfeld* birthed many memorable characters and phrases during its award-winning nine seasons. The Soup Nazi, and his famous line, have become ingrained in our collective psyche.

If you somehow missed out on the *Seinfeld* experience, here's a quick synopsis: A new soup stand opens in New York City, offering various soups that are out of this world. The proprietor, though, is an extremely rigid and unforgiving man who has a strict procedure that must be followed in order for someone to be allowed to make a purchase—earning him the nickname "Soup Nazi."

One mistake, one hesitation, even a simple question, would elicit those four most-feared words: "No soup for you!"

The Soup Nazi makes for great comedy, yet certainly we all agree that he is not someone we should emulate. Why does it appear, then, that the Soup Nazi has become our model of Christian conduct?

Across the good ol' "Bible Belt," we Christians are acting like we are God's store managers. We closely guard our (er . . . *God's*) merchandise and are wary of selling it too cheaply. We put a high price tag on items such as mercy, forgiveness, acceptance, and grace. And, with smug self-righteousness, convinced that God will be pleased with the strict efficiency with which we are running the store, we are engaging in an orgy of legislation to give us the privilege of boldly declaring, NO SOUP FOR YOU!

We Christians are doing so because we believe our faith is under attack. We've clearly identified the enemy (which naturally makes them *God's* enemy) who is attacking us: LGBTQ persons and anyone advocating for LGBTQ equality.

Thankfully, we can find in our Bibles solid instructions for us to follow in times like these. Are we confused about what we should do? Jesus gives us clear, concise guidelines. But we have to pause from weaponizing the Bible long enough to read what's inside.

Let's ask the Lord how we should treat people whom we think are out to get us, people we don't like, people whose behavior we have decided violates our own sense of personal morality. Not surprisingly, Jesus has an answer: "Just as you want people to act towards you, you act that way towards them." (I refer you to Luke 6:27-38, for example.)

Okay, Lord, we need to be more specific—we believe a certain group of people is our enemy and they are out to get us. "Love them," Jesus says.

"But they hate us and everything we stand for and believe in!" Jesus' reply? "Deal kindly with them."

"But Lord, we feel we are being insulted, even persecuted!" Jesus responds, "Well, then pray for them."

"But Jesus, by law we might have to do something that actually *enables* them!"

Jesus tells us that if, by legal requirement, we have to stop what we're doing and go out of our way to help an oppressor carry his or her load for one mile, then we should see it as an opportunity to serve that person out of the humility and unconditional love in our Christian hearts and carry the load for a *second* mile (Matt 5:38-42).

Dismayed that Jesus might be suggesting we dare to go against our cherished religious convictions, we angrily ask, "You mean we should bake a wedding cake for a gay couple?"

"Yes, and throw in the *groom's cake* for free!"[1]

"But Jesus, if they're gay, then . . . ." Smiling, Jesus just walks off to let us work out what that means.

Jesus certainly has a way of challenging our "sincerely held religious convictions" with simple compassion, mercy, love, and basic everyday kindness, doesn't he?

And lest my Pauline brothers[2] object, remember the letter to the Galatians. Are we worried about laws that prohibit the free expression of our Christian faith? There are no laws that can be passed against the work of the Holy Spirit in our lives, which blossoms forth through our becoming more loving, more joyous, more peaceful, more patient, kinder, better, more faithful, gentler, and more *self*-controlled (it's *not* our Christian duty to control *everyone else*).[3]

That's right! *There are no laws* that can prohibit *anyone* from freely modeling Christ-like behavior toward another person. How do I know that? The Bible tells me so.

Considering the number of lesbian, gay, and transgender individuals who are devout Christians, and who are praying and singing and serving and leading in our churches every Sunday,[4] this whole "gays vs. Christians" dichotomy is an illusion. It is harmful, an unbiblical and un-Christlike illusion.

Enough, then, with all this "legal protection" nonsense, please.

If we're going to model ourselves after TV personalities, it should be Mr. Rogers, not the Soup Nazi. Singing "Won't you be my neighbor?" sounds much more Christ-like, don't you think?

---

1. It is my sincerely held religious belief that Jesus wants us to go the second mile and, in this case, bake a second cake.

2. And they are overwhelmingly *brothers* who also use Paul's letters to silence our sisters.

3. See Galatians 5:22-23.

4. Whether or not the rest of us recognize it or not, LGBTQ folks have always been in the church.

Of Sex, Gender, and the Universe

(Or, My God! How Great Thou Art!)

Before he was even three years old, my young friend Jonathan became fascinated with the solar system. He could recite the names of each planet, in order, moving outward from the sun. He even included the dwarf planets!

Jonathan's curiosity called my attention to how much I take for granted about creation, about the heavens and the earth, and about God's majesty. Hanging out with Jonathan led me to stand drop-jawed in awe at the hugeness of God, and he reminded me of how little I really know or understand about the universe God created.

Scientists are always pushing the limits of our imagination as they "discover" new things that we've not known before. Physicists and astronomers and such are now discussing whether or not ours is a solo existence, or if we are in fact part of a "multi-verse"—one of *several* universes.

Even the most fundamentalist Christians among us today accept that the sun does not actually circle the earth and that the earth is not actually flat with four distinct corners.[1] Rather, when we, in awesome wonder, consider *all* the worlds God has made, our souls sing majestically with the great old hymn, "How great Thou art! How great Thou art!"

---

1. These things are in the Bible, after all. Maybe, instead of God dictating an inerrant book, the biblical authors wrote about their experience of God and creation based on their limited experience and limited understanding.

A fellow Baptist minister was called to meet and pray with a young couple. Their child had just been born, and the doctors were recommending surgery—the child had *both* male and female genitalia. The doctors could "fix" it, but the parents had to choose if they wanted a son or a daughter.

A Brown University biologist found that as many as 1 to 2 infants in every 1,000 births receive "corrective" genital surgery. Such surgeries are not medically necessary; rather, they are the result of social pressures to conform to an "either/or" binary understanding of sex.

Hearing my pastor friend share his experience with that couple and learning more about the not-so-uncommon occurrence of intersex births led me to stand drop-jawed in awe at the hugeness of God, and I was reminded of how little I truly know or understand about the vast diversity of God's creation.

Just as the world has always been round, and just as the earth has always been the third of several planets that rotate around the sun, we are coming to understand that throughout history, there has *always* been more to human beings than an exclusive binary system of being either male or female.

In Judaism, multiple categories regarding biological organs and gender expression are recognized in the Talmud. Native American cultures have long been aware of and embraced "two-spirited" individuals—people who are neither biologically nor socially distinctly male or female. And there is an ever-growing but already quite large branch of Christian theology that incorporates the spectrum of sex and gender (see Resources: Some Places to Start for a list of helpful websites and books).

Intersex and transgender people have always been with us—yes, even in our churches (we just didn't know it). Really, though, is it truly any of our business? Would *you* like it if everyone around you were suddenly concerned with discussing *your* genitalia?

Not unlike that time in our world so long ago when people began to challenge how we understood the earth and its relationship to the sun, many of us now are afraid. We're afraid that "new" information regarding sex and gender is a threat to God.

Sure, it may be confusing and overwhelming at first—growth spurts, whether physical, mental, or spiritual (or all three) always are. I still have trouble grasping eight, or possibly nine, planets, let alone trying to imagine a multi-verse instead of a universe.

By God's grace, some friends and students have trusted me enough to share privately with me their personal stories as transgender individuals. They have *very real* reasons to be afraid; they experience real threats all the time—threats to their families, to their jobs, to their friends, to their safety. These threats are made out of ignorance, plain and simple. Scientific ignorance and theological ignorance. Unfortunately, such ignorance is often encouraged, celebrated, and, some might say, idolized by the church.

But God is not threatened by any of our "discoveries" or advancements in human knowledge. The church should be the *safest* place for transgender individuals, and the church should be marching alongside scientists, leading the way as we continue to expand our knowledge about the vastness of God's creation. After all, it is science, along with the Holy Spirit, that is always pushing and prodding and pulling us beyond our cherished certainties and out into the wild mysteries of the universe until, with wide-eyed amazement and drop-jawed wonder, we humbly declare, "My God! How great Thou art!"[2]

---

2. If you need a moment to listen to Elvis's definitive rendition of this hymn, go ahead. The book will be right here when you get back.

A Kiss of Solidarity

(Or, When a Picture Is Worth Far More than Thousands and Thousands of Words)

A picture is worth a thousand words, they say. Recently, I learned just how true that is.[1]

I have written thousands of words over the past several years about how the church has failed our gay and lesbian family members, friends, and neighbors, and why I, as a minister of the gospel, seek to welcome and affirm and fully include everyone—both in the church and in civic life. Not only are my words written for all to see, but I have spoken such messages to groups, on panels, and from pulpits. Thousands and thousands of words.

When I recently asked a friend not to publicly post a picture of a Christian brother and me goofing off in which he puckered up and I leaned in and kissed him on his cheek, I had no idea how hurtful my request would be.

In the context of a fun evening at a church fellowship, when people were posing for pictures, the picture in question was taken. Later, I asked the photographer not to post the photo of "the kiss"; my reasoning was that, while it was quite funny to us, it might not be good for public viewing. I figured that people outside of the evening who didn't know the context would criticize not just me as a pastor but also the church and people in the church. My motive was to protect everyone—after all, it was just silly fun anyway.

Though I didn't know it, the picture had already been posted. After my friend received my request, she immediately deleted the photo. A few days later I learned how important that picture was to some

---

1. This musing is borrowed from *Of Mice and Ministers* (Macon: Smyth & Helwys, 2014).

friends of mine. What was done in the spirit of fun on the spur of the moment, it seems, had significant meaning to others. My credibility increased as a minister among my friends in the LGBTQ community because, to quote one of the comments I received, "it was awesome that a straight pastor would be cool enough to jokingly have kissed another guy."

When the photo disappeared, and inquiring minds discovered that I requested it not be posted, my credibility sank. The impression my action gave was that I was afraid of "looking gay."

One friend wrote to me, "It feels like someone thought there was something inherently wrong with the photo . . . ." Meaning that it is one thing to say it is okay to be gay, but that doesn't mean much if my insecurities cause me to worry about people thinking I am gay.

Another friend wrote to me, "I think it would be good for people to know how these things can harm. I know it's something that most people in the church wouldn't understand, but the fact is most people in the church have never felt physically unsafe because of the way they look. Most people in the church have never been harassed in a bathroom. Most people in the church have never spent more time on a date looking over their shoulder than enjoying their date. And I think it is important for straight people to understand that what they might think is a bad thing can actually make others feel safe, even if it's something small like a silly photo."

That last sentence is the one that hit me the hardest. "It is important for straight people to understand that what they might think is a bad thing can actually make others feel safe, even if it's something small like a silly photo."

I have always liked to think of myself as an advocate for and an ally of those on the margins, a person willing to stand in solidarity with anyone feeling left out, and especially with those being forced out and treated unequally and unjustly. It is at the core of my faith—that just as Jesus identified himself with the outcasts, so should we as Jesus' followers.

A simple request not to post a photo showed me just how far I am from reflecting the good news of Christ in my actions. All my thousands of words do not mean a thing if my actions keep me distanced from others, if they show my solidarity with the status quo rather than with those striving for equality.

Somewhere out there on the Internet is a photo of me jokingly kissing a friend. Nothing special, nothing serious, nothing but simple, light-hearted fun. But for my LGBTQ friends, neighbors, and members of my congregation, it is worth far, far more than even ten thousand words of support. It represents solidarity.

Besides, my friend and I were just doing what the Apostle Paul frequently instructs us all to do anyway: greet each other with a holy kiss.[2]

---

2. Funny, isn't it, how the biblical literalists literally don't take Paul as literally as they literally claim they literally do? This is a perfect example. Are *they* afraid someone might think *they're* gay?

Eating "Mor Chickin" and Loving More People

(Ode to Chick-fil-A and LGBTQ Equality)

This column was written in 2011, then reappeared in 2012 prior to Chick-fil-A's public statement that their tradition "is to treat every person with honor, dignity and respect—regardless of their belief, race, creed, sexual orientation or gender" (What a wonderful statement!). Mr. Cathy went to be with the Lord in 2014. Still today, however, I hear strong arguments for and against eating at Chick-fil-A. And still today, I try to practice the sentiments expressed herein.

You have probably heard by now that the delicious and fun fast-food chain Chick-fil-A is endorsing a marriage seminar held by a group opposing homosexuality. As a result, gay-rights groups are beginning to respond, and some college students are getting fired up and trying to push the "non-welcoming" restaurants off their public and diverse university campuses.

I do not think we need choose between our beloved waffle fries and our beloved gay friends. As an ordained Baptist minister, I do not think we have to choose between a company founded on Christian values and many gay friends whose deep Christian faith often outshines mine. In fact, when some of my gay friends come talk to my classes about their faith and being LGBTQ persons, we often follow it up with a delicious lunch at, of all places, Chick-fil-A.

Chick-fil-A founder Truett Cathy, I understand, was raised Southern Baptist. I, too, was raised Southern Baptist. And several of my gay Christian friends were also raised Southern Baptist (two of whom attended a prominent and respected Baptist college; and one of them served as president of the Baptist Student Union). Therefore, I want to reach out to both sides and begin appealing to our Baptist commonalities and to our sincere desire to follow Jesus.

To Mr. Cathy and the good folks at Chick-fil-A, let's be honest—we all know that Chick-fil-A frequently serves and even employs (though perhaps unknowingly) LGBTQ persons. So, with one hand the company publicly supports an anti-gay organization, while with the other hand it enjoys profits from the patronage of gay customers (and quietly from the labor of some gay employees). If gay money is good enough for your business, why aren't gay people good enough for your friendship?

To the good folks calling for protests and boycotts of Chick-fil-A, we all know that the employees we encounter are good local people who are working hard to make ends meet; they couldn't care less if they are handing a chicken sandwich to a straight or gay customer. While wanting to get the attention of the folks up in corporate headquarters, let us not take our attention away from our neighbors taking pride in their work.

Maybe there is an alternative to boycotting Chick-fil-A. Maybe the LGBTQ community and allies and friends could instead wear rainbow buttons and Pride T-shirts and go en masse to our local Chick-fil-A. We could practice the Golden Rule by bombarding the restaurant chain with increased business—supporting the local workers and employees (our neighbors and friends), and being visible agents of God's transforming and redemptive love, all while enjoying the tasty chicken strips and friendly service. You know, we might just be living examples of what the Apostle Paul describes in Romans 12:17-21 (look it up).

Maybe we could invite our Christian brothers and sisters who oversee the Chick-fil-A company to choose their corporate investments more wisely. Rather than their choosing to publicly support agencies that promote discrimination against and demonization of our neighbors, we can remind them of the Way of Jesus—that of loving our neighbors and that of doing to others what we would want done to us. There are some great organizations that partner with God in caring for others: Habitat for Humanity, Bread for the World, and Heifer

International, to name just a few. These are Christian groups that feed the hungry, house the homeless, and work to create a world in which we "let justice roll down like waters, and righteousness like an ever-flowing stream" (Amos 5:24, NRSV).

To Mr. Cathy—from one Christian to another, we must remember that our gay friends are created in God's image, too. If it would help, let's all get together for lunch at one of your Chick-fil-A locations. You bring some corporate leaders, and I'll bring a few of our LGBTQ Christian family members; we'll get to know one another, see names and faces and hear each other's stories, and we'll break bread (er . . . *chicken*) together, united in the bond of love.

And, by the grace of God, may our actions bear witness to the reconciling work of Jesus our Lord in the world today.

The Church and the New Civil Rights Movement

(Ode to Dick Brogan)

Richard "Dick" Brogan was a personal friend, and he was one of my heroes.[1]

Dick was a white Mississippi Baptist minister who worked tirelessly to build relationships between whites and blacks during segregation and even up until he passed away in 2011. Not so long ago, Dick was followed, harassed, threatened, and derided as a "nigger-lover" because he not only dared to speak against segregation but also dared *to act* as if in Christ there really is no Jew or Greek and no black or white.

Shortly before he died, Dick, a veteran of the civil rights movement, said that gay rights is today's gospel movement. I believe he was correct.

Consider the role of black churches in leading the civil rights movement and the role of many white churches in resisting it (isn't anyone disturbed that we *still* have to have "black churches" and "white churches"?).

Though Rev. Dr. Martin Luther King, Jr., and other black ministers found liberation and hope in the Bible, some white preachers remained silent, while many others openly preached segregation and racial inequality as biblically sound.

"Red birds do not fly with blue birds," white Christians smugly joked; "it's just the natural order of things."

With a clear conscience, many white church deacons and Sunday school teachers witnessed (and some *participated in*) lynchings, cross

---

1. This musing also appeared previously in *Of Mice and Ministers* (Macon: Smyth & Helwys, 2014).

burnings, bombings, and mob violence against marchers and sit-in participants. Stories abound in Mississippi of deacons at white churches armed with guns to protect the dignity of worship *for the white folks within.* They were simply defending "the way God intended things to be." After all, black people were tolerated just fine as long as "*they* stayed in *their* place."

A Baptist Broadman Commentary from 1970 reminds us that "The people of God are called to renewal in each successive era of their existence." In the 1950s and 1960s, Baptist preachers such as Rev. King and Dick Brogan followed the leadership of the Holy Spirit and called the people of God to renewal in a new era of their existence. Through them, God was transforming the religious life of God's people, often meeting the greatest resistance through the "guardians" of the Truth and the Faith.

Jesus pleaded with the religious establishment of his day, according to the Broadman Commentary, to "open the life of Israel to the power of the work of the Holy Spirit." The larger religious community's response to Jesus was his crucifixion.

And so King, Brogan, and others made the same plea. The responses to them were death threats, violence, exile, and, for King, assassination.

We are in the midst of another renewal; we are in the midst of another set of leaders pleading with the guardians of the Christian establishment to open the life of the church to the power of the Holy Spirit already at work; and some of the same words are being exchanged and variations of the same expressions of hatred are emerging in response.

There are a growing number of "gay churches" and welcoming and affirming groups pleading with the larger Christian community to recognize the movement of the Holy Spirit among the gay and lesbian community. And many of the long-standing institutionalized "straight churches" are actively resisting the work of God among those whom the "religious guardians" insist are not worthy. (One day, our grandchildren may sigh and ask why there have to be "gay churches" and "straight churches.")

"*They* want their children to go to school with *our* children! *They* want to live in the neighborhood *we* live in! *They* want the same rights *we* have!"

"God created Adam and *Eve*, not Adam and *Steve*," some Christians smugly joke; "it's just the natural order of things."

And with clear consciences, good churchgoers will openly bully, harass, and tease their gay neighbors, trying to get the gays to repent, to change, or to return to the closet ("to keep *them* in *their* place").

Despite what almost every single church sign says, openly LGBTQ people are *not* welcomed in most churches across the South and even across America. There may not be deacons armed with guns to keep *them* out and to *protect the dignity of the worship service* for the righteous folks within, but Sunday school lessons, book studies, and sermons bully *them* either to stay in the closet or stay out of the church.

When bullying leads to severe depression, psychological distress, and suicide, the church at large—at best—sits in silence. At worst, it leads the attack. Too many Baptist pastors are pressured to stay quiet on the issue while other Baptist pastors continue to verbally terrorize the LGBTQ people sitting quietly in their pews, living quietly in their families, and working quietly in their communities.

Dick Brogan was right: gay rights are today's civil rights. To paraphrase the great civil rights song, "deep in my heart, I do believe" that blacks and whites and gays and straights *will* walk hand in hand someday.

Why I Am a "Welcoming and Affirming" Baptist

A few years ago I sat on a discussion panel at one of the Baptist institutions of higher learning where I once studied.[1] The other panelists and I shared our thoughts as we explored this question: "Can someone be a Christian *and* be gay?" The following is a brief synopsis of why I answered with a resounding "yes!"

Let's recall a few basic facts about the earliest believers in Jesus, that community of believers in Jerusalem:

• They existed as a small group within Judaism. They were Jews who believed Jesus was the promised Messiah,[2] and they still worshiped in the synagogues and in the temple.
• They kept, or at least gave verbal allegiance to, the Law of Moses— things like not eating shrimp or anything from pigs and, of course, all the males having "a little minor surgical alteration" to mark them as God's people.
• They "knew" what God was like; they "knew" how to live in a "right relationship" with God; and they "knew" that God would not[3] act against what they practiced based on the authority of the Scriptures.
• They were not very fond of Gentiles (anyone who wasn't a Jew); their actions essentially said, "To hell with the Gentiles."

---

1. You may have also read this one before in *Psychic Pancakes & Communion Pizza* (Macon: Smyth & Helwys, 2011).

2. Only for the Jewish people, of course.

3. "God would not" as used here means "God *could* not!"

Now, to be fair, if a Gentile wanted to become a believer in Jesus, that Gentile could convert to Judaism, learn all the God-ordained actions of what to eat and what not to eat, and, of course, the males would have to get that "little surgical alteration." Then, and *only* then, a Gentile could become a follower of Jesus, the Jewish Messiah, and be in a "right relationship" with God.

There's a story in the eleventh chapter of Acts about some rebels who had the *chutzpah* to go forth into foreign lands preaching the gospel of Jesus Christ to . . . the *Gentiles*! Worse, these heretics let Gentiles respond to the good news without first converting to Judaism!

The believers back in Jerusalem had to take action; they had to defend the faith against such false practices. They sent Barnabas out to Antioch, with a letter of correction in hand, to investigate the situation and set everyone straight.

When he got there, though, Barnabas recognized the movement of the Holy Spirit, the power of the gospel of Jesus Christ, and the working of God *outside of* and even *in contradiction to* so much of what the Jerusalem believers "knew" to be true. Barnabas stayed among those Gentile believers for a while, and it was in Antioch, among those who were undoubtedly "getting it all wrong" and not truly in "right relationship" with God, that followers of Jesus were first called "Christians."

Now then, let's review a few basic facts about Baptists in America:

- We are ethnically Gentiles and not orthodox Jews. Many of us eat shrimp and pork products as freely and liberally as we desire.
- We are most certainly not overly concerned with which males have had that "little surgical alteration" (a procedure that, in America, has nothing to do with being God's chosen ones).
- We are the beneficiaries, then, of the early "heretics" who dared to recognize God's movement *outside of* and *even in contradiction to* what the Jerusalem believers "knew" to be true.

We Baptists are now in the position of the early believers in Jerusalem. We have become so enslaved to our own understandings that we "know" what God will not (meaning *cannot*) do. We have labeled an entire group of people "Gentiles," separating them from us, while our actions essentially say to them, "To hell with you."

We insist that LGBTQ people must first conform to what *we* say and do before they can grow in a relationship with Jesus. In other words, we need to correct *their* errant ways, and, well . . . set everyone *straight.*

Some of us, though, have witnessed the movement of the Holy Spirit among and the power of the gospel of Jesus Christ within our gay friends. Some of us have experienced the working of God *outside of* and *even in contradiction to* the teachings and doctrines of the Baptist tradition.

Like Barnabas, I choose to be open to God, whose love endures forever, whose mercy knows no barriers, and whose grace is far greater than my limited understanding, my feeble interpretations, and even my most certain beliefs of how to live in a "right relationship" with God.

We Baptists are being confronted today with the reality that God moves in ways that we are convinced God is not supposed to move—that God is, truthfully, bigger than and free from everything we "know" to be right.

This is why I am a "welcoming and affirming" Baptist—embracing, worshiping with, and serving alongside my LGBTQ brothers and sisters.

Part 3

The *Sermons*

Of Course, You'll Have the Good Taste Not to Mention that I Spoke to You

Sermon Text: John 3:1-17

You may have already recognized that the sermon title is taken from one of the greatest, most socially relevant, and downright funniest movies ever made: Mel Brooks's *Blazing Saddles*.[1]

An elderly woman in a small, Old West, all-white town is greeted by the newly appointed black sheriff: "Good mornin', ma'am! And isn't it a lovely mornin'?" Her racist and crude reply cannot be repeated from the pulpit.

Later, under the cover of night's darkness so as not to be seen, the old woman taps on a window behind the jail, apologizes for her remark, and gives the sheriff an apple pie. Then, she politely imparts, "Of course, you'll have the good taste not to mention that I spoke to you."

Social customs, family values, and religious expectations often restrict natural curiosity; they often hinder the asking of questions; and sometimes they threaten to punish with exclusion (or worse) those among us who associate with "the wrong people."

---

1. Written for and delivered to University Baptist Church, Starkville, Mississippi, on March 12, 2017.

In John 3:1-17, we read about a man named Nicodemus. Nicodemus is a scholar of the Scriptures. He is a teacher of the Jewish faith and tradition. He is a Pharisee. He is a member of the Sanhedrin (the Jewish ruling council).

Nicodemus, like the elderly woman in *Blazing Saddles*, visits Jesus quietly and under the cover of darkness. Whether or not he takes with him a freshly baked apple pie, we do not know.

Nicodemus could lose everything if he is seen talking with this heretical rabble-rouser named Jesus who is stirring up trouble among the common people. (John places this encounter just after Jesus has disrupted the moneymakers' corrupt transactions in the temple.) Nicodemus, however, is intrigued with Jesus; he *senses* something; he can't explain it. It's a deep—very deep—*tug* within his soul.

And, much like our Lord still does today, rather than giving Nicodemus all the answers to his questions, Jesus leaves him with more questions. Jesus talks about being born of the Spirit. Jesus talks about the wind blowing where it wills.

Nicodemus wants to believe, but his mind, his knowledge, his experiences, and his tradition are unable to help him process what Jesus is saying. It doesn't compute. It's like they're speaking in two different languages. Jesus did, though, have the good taste not to mention that Nicodemus had spoken to him.

By reading further into John's Gospel, we know that Nicodemus returns to his day job, but something is different. A man who is supposed to know all the answers, who is expected to understand and communicate God's message and teach God's ways to the people . . . this man is left with mysterious, nonsense ideas echoing in his head, in his heart, in his soul. He is left to toss and turn in bed at night, losing sleep, as he wrestles with all that Jesus said to him.

The message of John 3, of God's all-encompassing love for the entire world, is one that can get us into a lot of trouble. It counters everything we hold dear in the little territorial groups that we form in the name of God. It was a threat to the good, upright, religious folks of whom Nicodemus was a part (which is why he approached Jesus at night). It is why Jesus got into so much trouble.

Jesus lived out the scandalous truth of God's love for the world. In Jesus, God so loved a Samaritan woman—her ethnicity was supposed to exclude her. In Jesus, God so loved a paralyzed man—his paralysis was supposed to be a sign of God's judgment for his sinful behavior. In Jesus, God so loved a man born blind—his lack of sight was supposed to show the world God's curse for his sins or even the sins of his parents. Over and over and over again, Jesus demonstrated God's love, grace, mercy, and acceptance to those who were, by the "proper" interpretations of the Law of Moses, supposed to be far beyond God's reach, even God's concern.

Today, the social forces that prompted Nicodemus to find Jesus alone at night are still very much alive and well. They are still threatened by the Spirit of God blowing wherever it will, without their approval. They are still being offended that God *dares* to love the people they know God should not love, the people they are most certain God *cannot* love.

It is hard for all of us to comprehend the wideness of God's mercy and the depth of God's grace. Each of us finds it difficult to accept God's forgiveness without boundaries, to accept God's love without any strings attached. The greatest threat to our "sincerely held religious beliefs" is rooted in our favorite Bible verse: For God *so loved* the world—the whole entire world and everyone in it! (John 3:16)

Over the last several years, I have had encounters with curious students and others in the Starkville community: emails marked "private"; soft-spoken, whispered conversations; phone calls; meetings in quiet places. These individuals are like Nicodemus. They *sense* something, a tug from deep within. They want to know about our church that loves and accepts and is not threatened by our Muslim and Jewish neighbors. They want to know about our church that seeks to participate in racial justice and equality. And, more often than not, they want to know about our church that openly welcomes, affirms, and fully includes LGBTQ people.

I have been thanked many times for UBC's visible witness in our community. People tell me that UBC reflects the heart of God, that God's truly amazing love and boundless grace are evident in our fellowship. And yet, for any number of social reasons, being associated with our fellowship could get them in a lot of trouble.[2] And, of course, I try to have the good taste not to mention that they spoke to me.

---

2. We even have T-shirts that say: "UBC—the church your mother warned you about."

Cowardice, Courage, and the Chance to Love Boldly

Sermon Text: John 18:12-27

Back in 1979 and 1980, as I was approaching middle school, my musical tastes were expanding from Elvis and the Beatles into hard rock and heavy metal.[1] With KISS having been an entry point, thanks to my older cousin Jeff, I moved quickly into Iron Maiden, AC/DC, and, of course, Ozzy Osborne. So, whenever I lean in, turn my right ear toward you, and ask you to speak up, now you'll know why.

My parents, though, kept the radios at home and in the car tuned to country music stations. And in 1979 and 1980, Kenny Rogers songs were being played just about all the time on every country station and even on some pop stations. It felt like every second or third song played was his big hit "The Coward of the County."

Naturally, I couldn't stand Kenny Rogers. I mean, when you are an eleven-year-old middle-class white kid, a middle-aged white guy with all your friends' mothers swooning over him was just about as *un*-rock-and-roll as you could get. As I grew a little older, though, and became less concerned about presenting a hard rocker image to the world, I had to admit that Kenny Rogers sang some really great songs that told some really great stories. Like "Coward of the County," for example.

---

1. This sermon was written for and delivered to University Baptist Church, Starkville, on March 4, 2018—the Sunday before another Tuesday night meeting of Starkville's Board of Aldermen in which the Pride parade would be brought up again for a revote.

Have you ever listened to the lyrics of that song? It is a tragic, violent song about a horrific sexual assault: three brothers attack and rape a man's wife in her own home. Then the husband seeks and gets his revenge in a public place. But, as the chorus reminds us, everyone had always considered that husband to be the *coward* of the county.[2]

"Cowardice" is defined as the lack of courage to face danger, difficulty, opposition, pain, etc. In the Gospel text from John, Peter is acting cowardly. John juxtaposes Peter being interrogated with Jesus being interrogated. Peter's fears, insecurities, and knee-jerk responses for self-preservation in the face of danger, opposition, pain, and threat of death stand in clear contrast to Jesus' moral strength and bold presence for the sake of those he loves, even in the certainty of great opposition, danger, and threat of death.

Peter, who was always the first to jump up and declare his total allegiance, who was always trying to build himself up in the eyes of Jesus and in the eyes of the other followers as the most dependable, the most loyal, the most ready to fight and die for Jesus; Peter, who, when facing ridicule and scorn from the crowds and when facing all the opposition and power of the institutional religion and its leaders (what would be for us today the opposition and power of the institutional church and its leaders), and when facing the actual, real threat of jail and punishment and death, hid behind lies. Peter put on masks. Peter pretended to be something he was not to save his own skin. Peter was always ready to talk a big game, but he cowered in fear when it was time to perform.

Jesus, however, stood firmly and boldly, knowing full well what was coming. He felt no need to explain anything—except to say that his life, his actions, and his ministry all speak loudly and clearly. Besides, his interrogators who were demanding answers had already made up their minds. Nothing Jesus could have said or tried to explain would have convinced them otherwise. As John's Gospel records these events, at this point, by the time Jesus is brought to the high priest, he has already been condemned to die.

---

2. Heavy metal lyrics are quite tame compared to some of Kenny Rogers's tales!

Steve Thomason, a theologian and pastor who reflected on this passage from John's Gospel, asked, "How often do we put on the mask of someone else's story to save ourselves? . . . Three times Peter puts on a cover and hides behind a mask—protecting his true self, his real identity, and denying Jesus."[3] Like Peter, Thomason says, we also hide our identities, pretend to be something we are not, deny who God created us to be. So what do we do about it?

Thomason suggests a few things, and I want to share two of them. First, we should remember that we were created to be in community with others, in solidarity with one another, not to live for ourselves alone, that we were created to give ourselves in humility and sacrificially for the good of others rather than live for our own self-preservation at the expense of others. Second, we are called to live without fear. The spiritual journey is about becoming honest with ourselves and accepting and loving who God created us to be. It is about being real and honest with the world regardless of how the world responds to us. It is about no longer putting on masks to please others or to protect ourselves.

Thomason reminds us that we don't fool God with the masks we put on to try to convince God (and try to convince ourselves that we are convincing God) that we are better than we are or that we are not what we are.

Again, as I have been thinking about this text and preparing for this sermon, I have been doing so in the context of recent events in our community. For the past few weeks I have been, and still am, receiving emails from church folks across the region and from around the state demanding that I explain myself for supporting Starkville's Pride parade.

As we go into another Board of Aldermen meeting this Tuesday night, with the front page of our local paper and news reporters from around the country now watching, it is reasonable to expect pastors

---

3. All direct quotes from, and my summation and paraphrase of, Steve Thomason are from his sermon, "Peter's Denial—A Sermon on John 18:1-27," which can be found online at https://www.stevethomason.net/2018/03/09/peters-denial-a-sermon-on-john-181-27/.

and sisters and brothers in Christ to raise their voices against a parade that celebrates "those sinners."[4]

This is a time—a time for *us*—to face the loud and verbally aggressive crowd; to acknowledge that we know Jesus; to acknowledge Jesus in the very people being despised and condemned most; to recognize and align ourselves with Jesus; to see Jesus in the very people deemed to be the most beyond God's will, the least deserving of God's grace; to recognize and stand with Jesus among those our religious culture today deems "the least of these." This is our time to stand *with* Jesus, to stand alongside Christ *in* our family and friends and neighbors and one another.

After the resurrection, Jesus called to Peter and three times . . . three times! Three times, Jesus asked Peter, "Do you love me?" Three times. "Yes, of course," Peter answered. "Yes, I do." And, the third time, "Yes! You know I do." Peter made the "three times" connection.

After the resurrection, Peter became courageous. After the resurrection, Peter repeatedly learned to break with treasured religious traditions and risk the religious backlash. Peter went rogue with the Holy Spirit. Peter stood firm in the Way, the Truth, and the Life of Christ—regardless of the social pressures rising against him, even to his own death.

New Testament scholar Dr. Meda Stamper reminds us that Peter's story is *our* story. Peter's story shows us that there is hope for the "least bold among us,"[5] even in "our desperate lashing out and comfortable complicity and fearful denial."[6]

Peter's story shows us that there is hope for all of us who have hidden behind our masks, afraid of what might happen if our real selves, who we truly are, who we are truly created to be, our true identity, are discovered.

Like Peter, we too can be bold in Christ's love for all people; we too can be witnesses to the wildly inclusive, life-affirming love of God for this world and *everyone* in it.

---

4. It was a very reasonable expectation based on previous board meetings.

5. "Commentary on John 18:12-27" at https://www.workingpreacher.org/preaching.aspx?commentary_id=3406.

6. Ibid.

Because of a Pride Parade

(And Other Reasons I Believe in the Resurrection)

Sermon Text: John 20:1-18

I believe in the resurrection of Jesus Christ.[1]

As a young child, I believed in the resurrection of our Lord because I was told about it from the day I was born. At home, in church, in messages about it on church signs—the story was everywhere during the Easter season deep in the Bible Belt. I believed in it as a young child because I was taught to believe in it. A child's innocence, wonder, amazement, trust, and faith are powerful, glorious, beautiful, and life-affirming things, aren't they?

I believed in it as a child because of my innocence and childlike faith; and I believe in the resurrection today because of the joy, life, energy, laughter, love, and faith I see in children here at University Baptist Church, as well as in children everywhere. Our Easter egg hunt this Easter Sunday morning was overflowing with sign after sign after sign of joy and life and wonder and amazement. These are *resurrection* things!

Maybe that is why Jesus loved children so much and why he seemed to prefer having them around over the "adults in the room." Maybe that is why Jesus so harshly scolded adults for ignoring and neglecting children, and especially for crushing their spirits and sense of wonder and hope. *Woe to you who exploit, abuse, destroy, or simply ignore the beautiful, life-affirming joy, wonder, innocence, and trust of little children!*

---

1. Written for and delivered to University Baptist Church, Starkville, on Easter Sunday morning, April 1, 2018 (one week after the Pride parade).

I believe in the resurrection because I catch a panoramic view of it in the writings and the witness of Dr. Martin Luther King, Jr., and his stubborn insistence upon nonviolence and the transforming power of love and sacrifice over hate, ignorance, and death. I believe in the resurrection because it permeates page after page of Dietrich Bonhoeffer's writings and letters during the Nazi nightmare, even as he was approaching his own execution at Flossenbürg.

I believe in the resurrection because I, like some of you, have life-and-death and death-and-life experiences as described by Christian spirituality leader and writer Parker Palmer.[2] He writes boldly and honestly about the depths of his own depression, about his own suicidal tendencies, and about the direct contrasts with his own experiences of the sheer beauty and joys of life: "As an adult who's experienced death-in-life three times in profound depression, and was given the gift of new life each time—I know that resurrection in THIS life is a real possibility."[3] Palmer asserts that all of this says more about resurrection than anyone's statements of theology.

I believe in the resurrection because I have been privileged as a minister to be with women and men as they are dying. I have witnessed in some of them a tremendous peace that passes all understanding. I have seen their anticipation and joy. I have heard personal accounts of their glimpses of eternal light and the wonder awaiting them.

I believe in the resurrection because I witnessed it in such colorful beauty and splendor recently in Starkville's first-ever Pride parade. Listen to people's coming out stories. Listen to everyone who is willing to share their story. Each one is unique in its own way, yet there are common themes of darkness, coldness, fear, anxiety, and, for many (but certainly not all), feelings of defeat and despair, extreme depression, self-hatred, and suicidal thoughts (and attempts). Listen to the stories of having one's life, one's self, one's very being pushed and shoved deep down and hidden in shame to the point of being dead inside. Listen to the stories of coming out, of opening the door and emerging into a new life—like Dorothy opening the door of her black-and-white,

---

2. He's a sociologist, too! No wonder I love him.

3. Do you follow Parker J. Palmer on Facebook? I sure do! This reference comes from an April 7, 2012, FB post: www.facebook.com/montybert/posts/329456447108084.

tornado-ravaged Kansas farmhouse and walking out into the majesty and wonder of all the bright colors in the land of Oz.

I have heard Christian sisters and brothers share with me how it was the Holy Spirit, the Living Christ, their faith in God, that led them out of denial and repression and fear and shame and into life as openly gay and transgender people. I have heard them speak of their personal experiences of the world trying to crush, exterminate, and bury the life and love within them. They've experienced living death inside a bodily tomb. And I have heard them speak of how the love of God in Christ has given them new life and how nothing has ever been the same since!

U2 has a great line—a nod to the biblical story of Noah—that says, "after the flood, all the colors came out."[4] All the spectacular colors of God's rainbow were out in full display in Starkville's Pride parade, and all the bright colors of LIFE are out in lives all around us and in the LIFE springing forth all around us this Easter morning!

Christian writer Anne Lamott, like so many before her, reminds us as Christians that we are Easter people living in a Good Friday world. She writes,

> All of my work in the last 28 years has been about becoming a resurrection story—slowly, painstakingly healing from the damages of childhood in a family where the parents didn't love each other; the damage this culture does to children who are different; how the love of God, through friends, slowly helps us be restored to the person we were born to be.[5]

Did you catch that? *The damage this culture does to children who are different.* And *how the love of God . . . slowly helps us be restored to the person we were born to be.*[6] Lamott reminds us that in the Living Christ, we are *all* becoming resurrection stories.

---

4. The song is "Beautiful Day" and appears on the 2000 album *All That You Can't Leave Behind.* It's a beautiful song, too!

5. Quoted by Corin Pilling in an interview for the British journal *Christian Today,* 13 September 2014 <www.christiantoday.com/article/anne-lamott-i-am-a-broken-person-and-a-resurrection-person/40153.htm> (accessed 4 June 2018).

6. Go ahead, take a break and dance to Lady Gaga's "Born This Way." You know you want to.

I believe in the resurrection because in my own life I continue to experience love overcoming hate, grace overcoming law, mercy overcoming condemnation, faith overcoming apathy, and life overcoming death.

God's Got His Mojo Workin'

(The Bluesy Gospel for all God's Chillun')

A seminary professor assigned me two New Testament Scriptures and challenged me to write a sermon in the language of the blues.[1] Being rooted in the wonderful musical tradition of the blues, then, this sermon freely uses gender-specific terms and "incorrect" grammar.[2]

Sermon Texts: Matthew 8:5-10 and Acts 15:1-9

These two biblical stories translate perfectly into the language of the blues: We got our *no-jo* workin', but God's got His mojo workin'![3]

Did you get that? We got our *no-jo* workin', but God's got his mojo workin'!

You know about mojo—as in Muddy Waters, Big Mama Thornton, and even Elvis. They all sang "Got My Mojo Workin'." Mojo is the hoodoo, voodoo, good-luck love charms, and other such things that spread your love and good grooves out to others and draw others' love and good grooves back to you.

But you may not know about *no-jo*. *No-jo* is the religious opposite of mojo. It means withholding your love and good grooves from others and refusing to accept others' love and good grooves back upon you.

No-jo is the way we try to exclude others from God's kingdom.

---

1. You can thank, or blame, Dr. David Adams for this.

2. I've delivered this a few different times, including in Jackson, Mississippi, with my good friend Benton Stokes playing behind me on piano, and in Memphis, Tennessee, with Joyce Cobb and the Joyce Cobb Trio.

3. Really, I think the entire message of the whole Bible can be summarized as "God's Got His Mojo Workin'."

Like when we good church folks look at others and say, "No way, Joe—ain't no way you're worthy to be with us." Like when we good church folks say, "No, Joe; No, Jane—your *kind* ain't welcome here."

We religious folks have been practicing our *no-jo* curse since the beginning of time. You know how we are. We set up our standards of measurement, which become our *no-jo* hand, pushing people away who don't "measure up." No, sir! No, ma'am! We don't want the "them" out there to be mixin' with the "us" in here, so we keep our *no-jo* workin'.

In the book of Acts, we learn that the earliest believers were still living within their rich Jewish tradition and, like all good religious folks, holding strictly to their standards when it was convenient for them and whenever it helped clearly define who is "us" and who is "them." We see these earliest believers workin' their *no-jo*: they say that every male "outsider" must be circumcised to become a "good" Jew, and every male "outsider" must be circumcised and become a "good" Jew *before* they can become a believer in Jesus.

Confused? That's okay. *No-jo* likes to make things as confusing and as complicated as possible!

But get this: some early believers start going out to where non-Jews live, sharing the love of Jesus with a whole bunch of non-Jews, and they allow them non-Jews to accept Jesus' good news without making them get circumcised first! Without making them convert to and practice the Jewish laws and rituals first!

So the "true" believers back in Jerusalem—those folks who fiercely defend their religious standards—they start workin' their *no-jo*. They tell those Gentiles who mistakenly believe they are believers in Jesus that they have been misled, that they are mistaken. They aren't really loved, accepted, and affirmed by God through Christ. Not without gettin' fixed first: a little snip *here* . . . a little dietary restriction *there* . . . .

Now, get this: because *no-jo* is a *no-go* against God's *mojo*, Barnabas and Peter get busy cleaning up all this mess! First, Barnabas is sent to Antioch to correct those Gentiles, but Barnabas witnesses the movement of the Holy Spirit among those very people! Among those very people whom the "true" believers back in Jerusalem say are mistaken!

Then there's Peter. Peter—himself a good Jew—essentially says to those early "must-be-a-Jew" believers back in Jerusalem, "God ain't looking at anybody's private parts; God ain't withholding any love from anybody simply because somebody ain't gettin' cut on."

Peter says, "Listen here, God's only looking *into* hearts; God ain't discriminatin' between Jews and non-Jews; God ain't distinguishin' between 'us' and 'them.'"

In other words, both Barnabas and Peter tell those Jerusalem folks, "Your *no-jo* ain't workin' here, 'cause God's got His *mojo* workin' here!"

But it ain't just Barnabas, and it ain't just Peter. Jesus himself says as much, too. There's that story from Matthew's Gospel—that story about the Roman officer (he certainly ain't no Jew!). That Roman army officer comes up to Jesus and asks him to heal his servant. Jesus offers to go to the officer's house to heal the servant, but the officer humbly declines. He holds Jesus in such high regard that he feels he isn't worth all that trouble; in fact, he believes that Jesus can just speak the word of healing right then and there, and the servant will be healed. Jesus is amazed.

Jesus is amazed!

And Jesus says to all his followers (who are of Jewish persuasion), "This '*non*-Jew,' this '*outsider*,' has displayed far greater faith than any *I* have seen in *all* Israel!"

Jesus says, "This '*non*-Jew,' this '*outsider*,' shows greater faith; he has far greater faith than all of you who think you know all about God and what God wants!"

Jesus doesn't even take the time . . . Jesus doesn't even bother to look . . . to see if the officer has been . . . Jesus doesn't need to take a peek under the uniform . . . Jesus couldn't care less whether or not this man is circumcised!

You see, good religious folks always get their *no-jo* workin' to keep people *out*, but God's always got His *mojo* workin' to welcome people *in*!

Oh, how we church folks like to get our *no-jo* workin'! Your skin color ain't the right skin color. Your baptism ain't the right kind of baptism. Your beliefs ain't as right as *our* beliefs. Your practices aren't as holy as *our* practices. Your hair's too long; your hair's too short. You're too rich; you're too poor. You've got too many piercings. You hang out with the wrong kind of friends.

Yep . . . we church folks always find a way to keep workin' *our no-jo*. But God's always going around us and workin' His mojo! And our *no-jo* is a *no-go* against God's *mojo*!

Now then, what group of folks today do we in the church label as "them"? What group of folks today do we in the church try our best to keep separated from "us"? Who is it in our world today that we insist must get "fixed" (or "circumcised") before we will allow them to be a part of "us"? Who is it today that our *no-jo* hand keeps pushing away?

Now, you know what I'm talkin' about. And if you don't know what I'm talkin' about, I'm about to tell you what I'm talkin' about.

I'm what they call a "Welcoming and Affirming" Baptist. That means I think Peter is right: God's only looking *into* hearts, and God ain't distinguishin' between "us" and "them." And, like Barnabas, I have witnessed the Spirit of the Living Christ moving in and among my friends, and I have seen the Presence of God acting beyond and even against our most cherished doctrines and our most sincerely held religious beliefs. And I believe that God ain't discriminatin' between "gay" and "straight."

I believe Barnabas and Peter are telling the church today, "Leave them folks alone and let them respond to the gospel of Jesus just as they are!"

I believe Jesus is finding deep, sincere faith among the LGBTQ community—greater even than among some of the most prominent protectors of Christian doctrine!

All that *no-jo* ain't working here, 'cause God's got His *mojo* workin' here!

Part 4

The *And Such*

Invocation Delivered at Starkville's Board of Aldermen Meeting

March 6, 2018

Starkville Mayor Lynn Spruill asked me to give the invocation on the night the Board of Aldermen were to revisit the vote denying the Pride parade. This was my prayer.

Our God,

You are the maker of heaven and the maker of earth.

You created each and every one of us in your image:
each and every one of us across our wonderful city,
each and every one of us gathered here in this room;
despite our different skin colors,
our different nationalities,
our different genders;
despite even our different creeds,
our different religious beliefs,
or our *lack* of religious beliefs.

One of the most primary, essential teachings of our Holy Scriptures,
going all the way back to the very beginning,

is that in the midst of this tremendous diversity,
You, God, are here,
because *we* are here;
and each of us bears your likeness within us.

As we gather tonight
to do the administrative work
of the City of Starkville,
with the great diversity
of our wonderful community
on full display,
may those of us
who claim the name of Jesus
live out the words of the great hymn:

We will guard each one's dignity,
And save each one's pride,
And they'll know we are Christians by our love.[1]

In the name of Jesus I pray,
Amen.

---

1. From "They'll Know We Are Christians" by Peter Scholtes. It's one of my favorite songs. And yes, I added extra emphasis to the words "save each one's pride."

"Conversion Therapy," Heaping Coals of Shame, and Another Look at Chick-fil-A

(Ode to Bailey and the Conscience-Prickers)

December 2018

To eat or not to eat . . . at Chick-fil-A; that is *still* the question. It continues to cause arguments among members of the LGBTQ community as well as among us allies. Seven years have passed since I wrote the open letter to Truett Cathy. Since then, he has, as we Christians rightfully say, gone home to be with the Lord. Seven years later, and I continue to eat at Chick-fil-A; although, I confess, I am more conflicted now than then.

In that open letter, I made a passing reference to Romans 12:17-21. In case you neglected to look it up at the time, that is where the Apostle Paul says in dealing with our enemies we must leave their judgment to God; our job is not to let others' evil conquer us. Rather, we conquer evil by going out of our way to do good to those we consider our enemies, and, in doing so, we "heap burning coals of shame on their heads." I have been tossing and turning at night and thinking a lot about this because of my dear friend Bailey.

Bailey, one of Starkville Pride's co-founders, is an active member of University Baptist Church. She is also a fierce Chick-fil-A critic and a passionate, compelling advocate for boycotting the chain. I know other such critics who insist we should boycott Chick-fil-A, but only casually. I know Bailey well, I trust and respect her judgment, and I love her deeply. Thus, she complicates things for me.

"Chick-fil-A should be a no-go for any person who remotely begins to say they support the LGBTQ community," Bailey explains. "If the Cathy family's stance on LGBTQ marriage equality isn't enough to make you want to not give them your money, you can follow the dollars you spend every time you purchase something from Chick-fil-A." She has done her homework, and she will lay it all out in front of you and not-so-happily go over it with you. I know this because she has done it with me. Sitting across a table from her, I could feel Bailey's blood boiling as she told me about one of the anti-gay "conversion" organizations supported by the Cathy foundation (or supported by the other anti-LGBTQ groups that Chick-fil-A supports).

For the record, many Christian groups, including the Southern Baptist Convention, which once boycotted Disney over Disney's corporate support of same-sex employees, have officially renounced such "reparative" or "conversion" programs that claim to "fix" or "cure" people from being gay.[1] The evidence is undeniable and overwhelming: such "treatment" not only does *not* work, but it is painfully cruel, and psychologically, emotionally, physically, and spiritually torturous. These programs are proven to do long-lasting harm. In fact, some of their own leaders have walked away from them after decades of leadership, and they have gone on to publicly apologize for the harm they have inflicted on others. These leaders have also joined in the public opposition to "conversion" programs. At the time of this writing, my research indicates that fourteen states have banned such "therapy." Numerous city and county governments across the country also have such bans. Among the many professional groups that discredit and oppose "conversion therapy" are the American Medical Association, the American Psychological Association, the American Academy

---

1. See Sarah Pulliam Bailey, "Evangelical leader Russell Moore denounces ex-gay therapy," Religious News Service, religionnews.com, 28 October 2014 <religionnews.com/2014/10/28/evangelical-leader-russell-moore-denounces-ex-gay-therapy/>.

of Pediatrics, the National Association of School Psychologists, the American Association for Marriage and Family Therapy, the American Psychoanalytic Association, the National Association of Social Workers, and the American Counseling Association.

Bailey can, and will, describe for you in disturbing detail the horrors experienced by teenagers, such as the well-documented threats to their physical safety and even to their very lives—the rates of depression, self-harm, and suicide dramatically increase among young LGBTQ persons in unsupportive environments. Bailey has talked with many young persons who have undergone such "treatment." You can do your own internet research about the unscientific, medieval, and sadistic forms of "treatment" used to "cure" someone from being gay—reputable, scientific, and verifiable material is prevalent and quite easy to find. For Bailey, refusing to eat at Chick-fil-A is personal: any dollar spent in the restaurant is money that will go toward opposing LGBTQ-equality, and worse, toward terrorizing frightened teenagers, who simply cannot *not* be gay, and who are sent to camps against their will.

Most of us either cannot see, or choose not to see, the monetary connection from our taste buds to a teenager's living nightmare. Most of us, myself included, remain safely and comfortably distanced from the sinful torment of God's beloved children.[2]

What a messy, sticky, deeply tangled web we live in. Every seemingly little thing we do connects us in enormous ways we can never imagine to people we may never know in parts of the world we may never see. The clothes we wear. The televisions we watch. The cars we drive. All the electronic devices we hold. We *have* to remain ignorant of the horrible (and preventable) labor conditions, unfair trade practices, environmental destruction, and corrupt political influence behind it all in order to enjoy our cheaper purchases, lest we collapse in despair. Yet the computer I use, the coffee I drink, the gas I buy, and the shoes I put on come at an often unimaginable human cost. Likewise, my favorite

---

2. The phrase "sinful torment" is used here to mean it is utter blasphemy to suggest that God hates any person or hates their sin so much that God's grace is insufficient. Woe to you who tell confused and vulnerable children that God will not love or accept them until they have earned it by not being gay! Jesus has some choice "woes" for you who do such things (see Matt 18:1-6)!

waffle fries and chicken strips throw beautifully and wonderfully made children of God to the wolves.[3]

However, despite all of this, many of my gay friends[4] continue to eat at Chick-fil-A. Melissa, a long-time UBC member and a vocal LGBTQ activist in town, eats at Chick-fil-A frequently. When asked why, she shrugs and says she does not have a good answer other than she's "just a bad gay who likes chicken."

I asked another UBC member, Janean, who was very involved in the Pride events, how she felt. She's a health enthusiast who typically avoids fast food in general, but will eat at Chick-fil-A occasionally when out with friends or coworkers. She knows that neither all people who eat at, nor all the people who work for, Chick-fil-A support what the corporation does. Janean tries to just "meet people where they are." She added that she recently went mountain bike riding with a Chick-fil-A franchise general manager. "Interestingly enough," said Janean, "we had more in common than not."

Finally, I contacted John Smid and asked for his thoughts. I met and got to know John as he was walking away from Love in Action—a "gay-conversion" program he had been directing for twenty years. He had also served on the national board of directors of another "gay-conversion" organization, Exodus International, for about eleven years. John has since left it all behind, acknowledged the futility of trying to "cure" being gay or trying to "pray the gay away," and apologized publicly for the harm he caused. John has also gone on to write a book about it all, appear on national news programs, start Grace Rivers Ministries, and marry the man he loves.[5]

John gave me four reasons he and his husband, Larry, enjoy eating at Chick-fil-A: great food at reasonable prices; great service; clean restaurants with a nice, modern design; and always-friendly staff. "If I were to check boxes, jot and tittle, on businesses I choose to support based on their religious convictions, or whom they support, or do not support," John said, "I'd have to avoid virtually every business for

---

3. In sheep's clothing, no less.

4. And Bailey's, too.

5. Learn more about John and his book about his journey, *Ex'd Out: How I Fired the Shame Committee*, at www.gracerivers.com.

one reason or another." He added, "I honestly don't think the owners of Chick-fil-A function with an attitude of hate. I have friends who know them personally, and they are really kind people, Evangelical, but kind."

Social change always comes slowly, and it takes pressure from all sides to make it happen. The vocal opponents of Chick-fil-A need to keep shouting. Thank you, Bailey, and thank you to all the Chick-fil-A boycotters, for raising your prophetic voices filled with righteous anger. You pull back the curtains and expose for everyone to see what our buying habits cause behind the scenes. The role of prophets is to make us uncomfortable, disturb our souls, prick our consciences, and shake us out of our ignorance and complacency. May we have ears to hear, eyes to see, and hearts to act.

For all of us who still patronize our local Chick-fil-A restaurants, though, we, too, can commit to play a redemptive role while enjoying our nuggets. There are countless ways in which we, as regular customers, can bear witness to the wildly-inclusive love of Jesus and constructively engage the chain's corporate leaders with Truth and Grace.

Here are just a few ideas:

First and foremost, always be kind, patient, and grateful with the employees at our local restaurants. There is never a good reason to be rude to hard-working folks trying to make a living.

Now then, since Chick-fil-A is not a tipping restaurant, every time you eat there, send a 20 percent tip to a local LGBTQ-affirming church or a national faith-based LGBTQ advocacy group. Each time, be sure to note that your gift is in honor of your eating at Chick-fil-A, to counter their funding of anti-gay groups. Include the Chick-fil-A corporate address in case your chosen organization wants to send a note informing Chick-fil-A of the donation.[6] I know a 20 percent tip on a Chick-fil-A meal isn't much, but it is the symbolism here that matters most, as well as getting in the habit of doing it every time you eat there. Besides, I am neither a literalist nor legalist you can always give more.

Also, when you eat at Chick-fil-A, you can send an online message to the corporate office through their website, or send a handwritten

---

6. Chick-fil-A, P.O. Box 725489, Atlanta, GA 31139-9923

note in the mail (see address in the previous note).[7] Start the note
with a compliment about the service and why you enjoyed your visit
to the specific local restaurant. Let them know that as a Christian, you
affirm the company's desire to be guided by the values of our faith.
Inform them that you just made a financial donation to an LGBTQ-
affirming church or organization in their honor (be sure to name the
specific church or group and give a website address; for variety, give
to a different group each visit). Finally, say that you are praying the
Holy Spirit will lead them to stop supporting anti-gay organizations
that cause spiritual and emotional harm to God's beloved LGBTQ
children.[8]

Yet another idea is for your Sunday school class or Bible study
group to do a monthly letter-writing campaign to the corporate office,
focusing on a particular faith-based LGBTQ group you would like to
see Chick-fil-A support instead. Or, perhaps your group can purchase a
number of various LGBTQ-affirming Christian books and send them
one-by-one as sort of "book of the month" ministry.[9]

As for me, I will begin to rotate among the above options each
time I visit, and I will make sure to join my friend Melissa at our
local Chick-fil-A from time to time. Melissa is, as she describes herself,
a "stereotypical 'butch' lesbian." In my correspondence with the
corporate office, and in keeping with Romans 12:17-21, I might even
include a photo of the two of us enjoying our meal together.

---

7. https://www.chick-fil-a.com/Contact-Support
8. Then, be sure to say that prayer with each email or note you send.
9. You'll hear no opposition from me if the company was inundated with
copies of this book.

Let's Talk about Sin . . . and Emails

I received more than a few emails in response to my column about Jesus and Starkville's proposed Pride parade. About half of them were positive, offering words of appreciation. They were, for the most part, short and to the point. Here are a few examples taken from some of those emails:

- "Thank you for your excellent piece in today's *Clarion-Ledger*. Your description of Jesus's love for all God's children . . . was very refreshing. It is an attitude I have found lacking among many people in Mississippi."
- "I couldn't agree more that Jesus would be carrying a rainbow flag in a pride parade if he could."
- "As a lifelong Methodist, straight, grandfather . . . I support and admire you for your courageous column."
- "As a Christian, lesbian, AND an Ole Miss fan,[1] I would like to THANK YOU! While your words may not reach everyone, maybe [they] will give some a little more compassion for their neighbor . . . God bless the work you do."

About half the emails, though, were not so appreciative. These negative ones were lengthy, angry diatribes. Here are just a few brief excerpts:

---

1. Nobody's perfect. Hail State!

- "I read with horror and disgust your article this morning. Shame on you for spewing such trash."
- "You, Sir, are no pastor! You are a wolf in sheep's clothing."
- "A Baptist 'pastor' celebrating sin! You are allowing homosexuals to hear a false gospel."
- "I cannot imagine going to your church. There is a special place in HELL for you. Who is one of your deacons? Let me guess— Madonna."

One Christian brother emailed me repeatedly for over a month.[2] Most of his messages were dissertations filled with Bible verses, sarcasm, and cut-and-paste excerpts from fundamentalist preachers. He accused me of "dereliction of pastoral duty" and warned that one day I will stand before a Holy God and have to answer for my heresies. Eventually, I assume after finding other columns of mine online, he concluded, "I'm slowly learning that you are a radical false preacher. You don't even remotely pretend to be a Bible-believing Christian. No wonder you write these heretical op-Ed's [sic]. I just thought you were not familiar with the Bible."

The essential difference between the positive emails and the negative emails boils down to whether or not being gay is a sin. By this point, you have probably figured out that I have long ago ceased viewing being gay as a sin; furthermore, I am absolutely convinced that the Bible—when we approach it seriously, reverently, and honestly under the guidance of the Holy Spirit—does not call it sin, either.

I want to say that again, and this time in bold print, so that I am as clear as I can be: **I have long ago ceased viewing being gay as a sin; furthermore, I am absolutely convinced that the Bible—when we approach it seriously, reverently, and honestly under the guidance of the Holy Spirit—does not call it sin, either.**

Before you begin demanding that I explain in depth how, and why, and what Bible verses I can show you . . . let me remind you what I wrote in my prologue: it is not my concern here to compose

---

2. Following the advice of more experienced pastors, I did not reply to any of his emails or give him any reason to believe I was interested in engaging him in an argument. Nevertheless, he persisted . . . for a while, anyway.

a detailed theological treatise. Nor is it the purpose of this book to examine in a scholarly, contextual manner the handful of Biblical "clobber passages."[3] Again, there are numerous theologically sound, biblically faithful resources out there that explore the historical and cultural context of Leviticus,[4] the original language and translation issues in both our Old and New Testaments, and exactly what Paul was addressing in his letter to the Christians in Rome.[5] If this is an itch you need to have scratched, you may find the Resources chapter (at the end of the book) helpful. It is nothing more than a short list of books and websites to help get you started in your studies.

Nevertheless, I do want to speak to three common questions/ themes that repeatedly popped up in the less-than-supportive emails:

1. Do I believe Jesus would support a parade that celebrated murderers, rapists, pedophiles, or even liars and gossips? Then, why a parade for homosexuals?
2. But, Jesus said / the Bible says, "Love the sinner, hate the sin!"
And,
3. Jesus would tell homosexuals the same thing he told the woman caught in adultery: "Go and sin no more."

First, I'll repeat that I am convinced by the leadership of the Spirit of Christ, through a lifetime of faith and biblical studies, and by meeting God in my LGBTQ friends, that being gay and being transgender are not sins against God. After all, we are, as Psalm 139:14 reminds us, "fearfully and wonderfully made." That being said . . .

---

3. "Clobber passages": those Bible verses used repeatedly and often to condemn, harass, attack, judge, and inflict emotional/spiritual pain, guilt, and shame upon LGBTQ persons.

4. One cursory reading through Leviticus will reveal how we conveniently dismiss as "no longer relevant" all the other restrictions and laws which relate to property, wealth, seafood, clothing, stoning children to death, or heterosexual sexual practices within marriage (to name just a *few*), while clinging tightly to those few verses that let us condemn homosexuality.

5. In short, Paul addressed the prevalent practices of rape, temple prostitution, pedophilia, and other forms of sexual exploitation. Consensual, loving adult relationships were just not on his list of concerns, if they were even on his radar.

(1) Do I believe Jesus would support a parade that celebrated murderers, rapists, pedophiles, or even liars and gossips? Then, why a parade for homosexuals?

I do not know where to start with this one, because even if I thought being gay *was* sinful, to compare a person's orientation or gender identity to killing someone or molesting a child just does not sound like Jesus. Not in the least bit. What *does* sound like Jesus, though, is talk of the heart and talk of relationships (see the Sermon on the Mount): all that stuff Jesus says about loving others as we love ourselves, doing unto others, etc. Sin is clearly failing to recognize or refusing to respect the image of God in any person, in all people. Sin is dehumanizing someone, objectifying someone, using and abusing someone as a means to your own selfish end. These are the sins in our hearts that lead us to bear false witness against one another to build ourselves up and tear someone else down. These are the sins in our hearts that lead to sexual exploitation and sexual violence against others, that lead even to committing murder.

This is the heart of the Ten Commandments, the Law of Moses, and all the prophets. This is the heart of the Way of Jesus. So, no, being gay is not a sin any more than being redheaded, or left-handed, or having dark skin, or even being a female is a sin. And, no, being gay is not the same as killing or raping or lying or any other sins that arise from the stuff in our hearts.

Several years ago, I met with a few people who asked why University Baptist Church welcomes and affirms LGBTQ persons, why we "allow" them to participate fully and even lead in worship. One Christian brother at the table said that if one of my church leaders was a violent alcoholic who beat his wife, then my responsibility would be to confront his sinful actions, call him to repentance, and help him stop drinking and abusing his wife. The same, then, is true for any homosexual who comes into my church: It is my calling and the church's responsibility to confront the sin, call them to repentance, and offer to help them stop being gay.

I responded by sharing with him about one of the healthiest, most loving and committed couples I know—Renee and Connie. I had known Renee for over 20 years (at the time), and the depth of her faith, her love for Jesus, and her love and knowledge of the Holy Scriptures have always inspired me.[6] I told my friend at the table that comparing Renee and Connie's relationship to the violent behavior of an alcoholic, wife-beating husband was not only detestable, but it was also ignorant. Such a comparison, I said, was itself sinful. And that leads us to the next one . . .

(2) But, Jesus said / the Bible says, "Love the sinner, hate the sin!"
I asked my old Union University classmate and friend, Monica, how she usually responds when she hears someone say, "Love the sinner, hate the sin." You need to know that Monica is a child of Baptist missionaries, was raised in Baptist churches and the Baptist faith and tradition, and still very much loves Jesus. Today, though, she serves our Lord as an ordained United Church of Christ chaplain. Oh, and she's a lesbian—happily married for almost 25 years (the last five years with her marriage legally recognized in her state of Minnesota). Monica's reply was quick and succinct: "'Tain't sin." Monica always knew how to get right down to the crux of the matter.

"Love the sinner, hate the sin." We can repeat it faster than we can recite John 3:16, Romans 6:23, or Psalm 137:9.[7] The problem is, Jesus did *not* say it. The Apostle Paul did *not* write it in any of his letters. Moses did *not* carve it into the tablets. King David did *not* sing it while playing his lyre. "Love the sinner, hate the sin" is *not* a Bible verse.

To be fair, whatever the origin of the post-biblical phrase,[8] it obviously draws upon several sentiments scattered throughout our Scriptures. Some are about God's wrath in response to sin. Some are about Jesus' love for people. Over time in our church history, the phrase eventually evolved into a neatly packaged quip ready for quick and easy use. It is like opening a package of instant oatmeal or preparing a

---

6. She was the student president of the Baptist Student Union at Mississippi College, after all. One does not become BSU student president at a Baptist college by being a slouch in the faith department.

7. OK, so we never actually learned this one in Bible drill. I just threw that in there to see who is paying attention.

8. Some have suggested that an early form of the phrase can be found with St. Augustine of Hippo, well over three hundred years after the time of Jesus.

cup of instant coffee; here, though, we have instant judgment. Yes, of course, I love you, *but* . . . and off we go on the judgment train.

We even consider the saying more authoritative than what Jesus actually does say in the Bible (things like not judging others, for instance). The trouble with "love the sinner, hate the sin" is that the second part always gets in the way of the first part. The second part grants us license to judge others; to hold something against someone else.

When I say it, I am saying there is something about *you* that blocks my ability to love you as God loves you; there is something about you that marks you as less-than, as undeserving, as not being good enough for my unconditional love. I will love you, but only so far, only with some conditions; there are limits. I am unable to see beyond what I consider your faults. I am unwilling to see you as anything more than what I do not like about you. No, I will not love you as God loves you, nor even as God loves me.

Perhaps we are so attached to "love the sinner, hate the sin" because we have yet to stop hating ourselves, our own sins, and we have yet to embrace God's unconditional love for us as we are. Yes, I know God loves me, *but* . . .

Something Jesus *does* say is, "Stop judging! Just stop it! If you love judgment so much, then you'll be the one that gets judged. Whatever standard you use to judge someone else, God will use to judge you!"[9]

In the Gospels according to Matthew and Luke, Jesus says we should pay attention to the big oak tree growing in our own eyes and distorting our vision. We get all worked up about something that looks like a speck in someone else's eye, but, truthfully, we can't see much of anything with all that timber sticking out over our noses and blocking our view. If we could see perfectly and without any obstruction, if we could remove the log in our own eyes, we might discover that what we thought was a horrible speck of dirt in another's eye in need of removal was really just a benign eye freckle.

Let's go back to my dinner with Christian sisters and brothers concerned about the people in the church where I pastor. One of them said that whenever he saw a homosexual, all he could think about—in

---

9. My paraphrase of Matthew 7:1-2 and Luke 6:37-38.

graphic detail—was the ways that man must be having sinful, gay sex. He was repulsed, therefore, just by being around someone who might be gay; imagine how hard it would be to worship with "practicing homosexuals" sitting next to him or reading Scripture at the pulpit. [10]

I asked him if he looked at all straight couples the same way— immediately imagining them being sexually intimate with one another. Does he think the only thing anyone sees of him is what he and his wife might be doing in their bedroom? Loving relationships, whether gay or straight, are so much more than mere sexual acts. If he is convinced that the church must be concerned with what two loving adults are doing in their bedroom, then he should be willing to start with private details of his marriage and personal sexual history. We all agreed that this was none of our business, and we didn't want to know. Neither, then, is it any of our business to imagine (then announce our disgust about) what any other consenting, loving adults are doing. If we can't let go of those images, and see instead persons bearing the image of God, perhaps it is we who need to repent and, yes, probably get some therapy.

And that takes us to the final recurring email theme:

(3) Jesus would tell homosexuals the same thing he told the woman caught in adultery: "Go and sin no more."

The eighth chapter of John's Gospel tells us the story we like to refer to as "the woman caught in adultery." I think we like to call it that because it allows us look at someone and clearly identify her as a sinner. Really, though, it is a story about Jesus confronting a self-righteous— and deadly—mob. Nevertheless, the familiar story gives us two great lines, both from the mouth of our Lord: "Go and sin no more," and, "You who are without sin cast the first stone."

Respectable religious leaders brought a woman to Jesus who had been caught in the very act of sexual sin. The male, the other participant in the act, was not at fault here; in Jesus' day, men did not have to abide by the same rules as women. God's law, as they interpreted and applied it, said the woman was the sinner, but the man was not.

---

10. My friend Melissa, a local leader in the LGBTQ community, says straight people seem to think a whole lot more about gay sex than gay people do.

Jesus moves away from the defenders and protectors of the faith and stands with the woman. Jesus stands alongside the person being judged. Jesus stands with the woman declared "sexually sinful" who is about to be killed.[11] Jesus stands with the person having Scriptures and righteous slogans hurled at her. Jesus stands with her, and facing the self-righteous and armed men doing their godly duty, says to them, "You who are without sin, cast the first stone."

Before we assume that Jesus would tell homosexuals, "Go and sin no more," let's pause for a moment. Let's read the story again. Slowly. If we are paying even the slightest bit of attention, we will see that *we* are the *accusers*. *We* are the ones calling out and identifying someone as a "sinner." *We* are the ones hurling self-righteous slogans and other verbal stones of condemnation at someone. *We* are the ones Jesus stands up against. Jesus deflects our holy pursuit of sinners right back upon *us*. If we insist on hunting out sin, then sin's scent is leading us directly back to our own hearts. It is that whole log/speck thing again.[12]

When we dare say, "Go and sin no more" as a way of commanding someone to stop being gay, we reveal our own laziness regarding both our faith and our study of Scripture. In the context of the whole story, "Go and sin no more" is Jesus' good news to the accused "sinner" that she is no longer under these religious leaders' condemnation. Their label of "sinner" has been removed from her; she is neither subject to her accusers' labeling nor their judgment. When we point fingers at LGBTQ persons and so smugly tell them to "go and sin no more," we fail to grasp the radical, liberating grace in Jesus' words. These are not words of judgment. These are words of freedom! The woman is set free from living, and in her case, dying, under the condemnation of religious "authorities." How ironic—and downright *sinful*—that we use Jesus' life-affirming words to pummel others with our judgment.[13]

Back to that dinner with folks asking questions about my church and me. One of them was explaining to me how I was wrong for "enabling homosexuals" to continue living in their sin. Did I not know

---

11. In accordance with God's commandments, of course.

12. Jesus sure knows how to ruin a good stoning.

13. I refer you back to Matthew 7:1-2 and Luke 6:37-38.

Jesus told the woman caught in adultery that she should *go and sin no more?*

It had been a long night. It may not have been my finest pastoral care moment, but out of sheer exasperation, I countered: "Well, how is that working out *for you?* When *you* have managed to successfully go forth and never sin again, let me know, and then we can talk about your advising others to do the same."

The Journey toward Affirming: An Invitation

(Or, We're Gonna Need a Bigger God)

J.B. Phillips was right: "Your God *is* too small."[1]

If there is a single recurring theme through all the musings, sermons, and such herein, it is that God is always bigger. Bigger than our most treasured doctrinal assertions and creeds, denominational statements of faith, favorite Bible verses, cultural traditions, and political or religious laws. Bigger than the walls we construct to block us off from one another. God is always so much bigger.

The way we learn this eternal truth is through one another; Jesus meets us in our relationships with others. All the things previously listed help distinguish us from others and help us form our individual and group identities, yet they also become barricades we erect to separate us from others. Barriers give us a sense of security, of protection, of certainty, of the "known." However, the only way to walk with Jesus more closely, to follow the movement of the Spirit more faithfully, to know God more fully, is to risk going through and beyond those sacred boundaries. It is a frightening, daring, and risky migration to walk into the unknown.

In many ways, the journey toward LGBTQ-affirmation is not unlike the existential odyssey described in our Old Testament book of Ruth. In fact, it can be encapsulated in Ruth 1:16:

---

1. If you have not read the almost-too-small book from J.B. Phillips, *Your God Is Too Small*, finish this book, then immediately do an internet search for that one, order it, pay for expedited shipping, and read it tomorrow. I am extremely thankful that my father introduced it to me when I was young, and that I grew up in a Baptist church in which the pastor and other leaders often referenced it.

Where you go, I will go;
   where you lodge, I will lodge;
your people shall be my people,
   and your God my God.[2]

Throughout this book, the emphasis has been on knowing people personally, on meeting Christ in others—especially those people who are supposed to be "on the outs" with God.[3] Until you allow yourself to have such a holy encounter, I doubt any amount of explanations, essays, or biblical investigation will change your mind about LGBTQ-inclusion.

In my early-to-mid twenties, two friends, whom I had long admired for the depth of their faith, came out as gay. I had known one of them, David, almost my whole life. He was a few years older than me, and I idolized him and longed to have the passion for Jesus that he had. The other, Renee, is a few years younger than me; we met at Mississippi College when I was getting my master's degree and she was finishing her bachelor's degree. The joy of the Lord shined brightly through her personality and in her life. Renee's love for Jesus was contagious.

Contrary to some popular beliefs, neither of them turned away from their Christian faith so that they could go be gay instead. In fact, their faith and understanding grew deeper and stronger as they learned to accept and love themselves as God already fully loved them, as God created them. This was my "Barnabas" moment[4] in which I personally witnessed the Holy Spirit freely moving within two people that the contemporary church tagged as "Gentiles."[5]

As I look back, it was then that I essentially said, "Your people shall be my people, and your God my God." It was then that I committed myself to walk in faith with my LGBTQ friends. And it was then that I learned just how narrow my view of God had been.[6]

---

2. The New Revised Standard Version.

3. And, who, therefore, should remain "on the outs" with us.

4. See "Why I'm a 'Welcoming and Affirming' Baptist" and "God's Got His Mojo Workin'."

5. See previous footnote.

6. And I was a fairly open-minded Baptist!

And, so, we return to the story of Ruth.

Renee and her wife, Connie, have matching wedding bands with the beautiful words from Ruth 1:16 engraved in the biblical Hebrew: "Where you go I will go; your people shall be my people."[7] These are indeed beautiful and powerful words of commitment and love of one to another. They are sometimes heard in traditional wedding ceremonies.

The larger Biblical story of Ruth, however, is about much more than marriage. Remember, these loving words are spoken by a daughter-in-law to her mother-in-law following a series of very unfortunate events: famine and starvation, leaving one's homeland and migrating to a foreign land, and death after death of the husbands that connected these women.

The book of Ruth is a story about immigrants, refugees, and strangers in a strange land. And, it is about people that God, by all accounts, was supposed to hate. The Israelites despised Moabites, and you know what Anne Lamott says about how God manages to hate all the same people we do.[8] The Moabites' very existence was viewed as an abomination. Though they were a part of Abraham's extended family, they were the descendants from Lot's incestuous union with his daughters. Therefore, for centuries and centuries, the Hebrew prophets reminded the people that God *hated* Moabites. The priest Ezra, a hyper-nationalist who never passed up a chance to demonize foreigners, was so concerned with the ethnic and religious purity of the Israelite people that he forbade the marrying of Moabites. The feeling was, understandably, mutual. In another favorite story from the Hebrew Scriptures, the king of Moab hired a prophet named Balaam to curse Israel. You remember the story of Balaam and his talking ass, don't you?[9]

---

7. That is *not* the Biblical Hebrew, but, as quoted earlier, the New Revised Standard translation.

8. The actual quote is, "You can safely assume you've created God in your own image when it turns out that God hates all the same people you do." Add Anne's *Traveling Mercies* to your reading list if you haven't read it already. In fact, just add Anne Lamott's entire library to your reading list.

9. The famous talking ass is found in Numbers 22:21-29.

In the book of Ruth, Israelites marry Moabites. Israelites live among and form trusting relationships with Moabites—all a deliberate violation of what was perceived as God's perfect social order. All of it was an affront to every single "sincerely held religious belief" among God's people. In fact, the heroine of the story for whom the book is named—who would become an ancestor of King David, then our Lord Jesus himself—is a Moabite.

This story is rich in meaning at so many levels, of course, and we cannot overstate its importance to this historical moment in our nation as we wrestle with xenophobia, nationalism, migration, immigration, and refugees. Nevertheless, I cannot escape the notion that there is a connection to the stories of all of us straight Christians who have chosen to journey with our LGBTQ family and friends, leaving behind the religious certainties of our traditions, some even being rejected by our denominational households, and finding ourselves on a theological migration toward a God who is so much more than we had ever known or imagined before.

Becoming a welcoming and affirming Christian does not happen after study and rational weighing of theological "facts." Study and analysis separated from genuine interaction with others will never change our hearts and minds. We become LGBTQ-affirming Christians through genuine, caring, trusting relationships with LGBTQ persons, regardless of what our study and religious "facts" tell us.

Like Ruth, the Moabite in her own homeland, who attached herself to her mother-in-law Naomi, an Israelite in the land of Moab, and then left Moab to journey with Naomi into a whole new world, Christians become affirming by committing ourselves fully to the gay and transgender persons we know and love; by refusing to let them make their journey without us; by willingly walking across, through, around, and beyond all our theological boundaries into the unfamiliar and unknown; and, by declaring to our LGBTQ family and friends, "Your people shall be my people, and your God my God."

The relationships with and commitment to LGBTQ persons comes first; the beliefs, interpretations, and theological adjustments or outright overhaul always comes later, along the way. During the journey we will discover our fears, worries, denominational flags, and theological weapons falling away; as we travel we will see our narrow, restrictive view of God crack and crumble. And soon, in awesome wonder, we will find ourselves standing within the wide diversity of God's beautiful kingdom, celebrating the wildly inclusive love of Jesus.

In true Baptist fashion, I end with an invitation to respond, written and sung by my friend, singer/songwriter Daniel Bailey:[10]

The Mountain is calling, "Travelers take to the road";
Ah, the Mountain is calling, "Traveler, it's time to come home."

I'll come home to find:

The God that is bigger than the sum of our deeds,
And the taker of fears, and the giver of dreams;
The God that is bigger than the plans that we have made,
Than the bombs in the sky, or the flags that we wave.

And, the Mountain is calling, It's calling to those who would hear,
"Turn your swords into plows, find the love that casts out all fear."

And you will find:

The God that is bigger than the sum of our deeds,
And the taker of fears, and the giver of dreams;
The God that is bigger than the plans that we have made,
Than the bombs in the sky, or the flags that we wave.

The Mountain is calling, It's calling out to us all;
Saying, "Build up the little ones, and tear down all of your walls!"

Tear them down to find:

The God that is bigger than the sum of our deeds,
And the taker of fears, and the giver of dreams;

---

10. "The Mountain" by Daniel Bailey, 2002. The only thing better than reading the lyrics is listening to Daniel sing them. They are used here, of course, with permission. (Thanks, Daniel!)

The God that is bigger than the plans that we have made,
Than the bombs in the sky, or the flags that we wave.

May it be so.

Homophobia Is Heresy

(An Epilogue)

I often joke about being a heretic. I've never been an institutional guy—religious or otherwise. Yet in all seriousness, people I know and people I do not know have felt compelled to call me a heretic. They warn that I teach and preach dangerous heresies that lead people astray. My insistence on LGBTQ acceptance and equality is most often submitted as Exhibit A.

Heresy, as defined by dictionary.com, is an "opinion or doctrine at variance with the orthodox or accepted doctrine, especially of a church or religious system." By that definition, I am certainly guilty, and I consider myself in pretty good company. Hey, if I may paraphrase Willie Nelson,[1] my heroes have always been heretics, and they still are, it seems: Thomas Merton, Will Campbell, Glenn Hinson, the Indigo Girls . . . even the biblical prophets, early church leaders (like Barnabas, Peter, and Paul), and, yes, our Lord Jesus Christ, were all considered heretics in their own time.[2]

I may be a heretic in relation to some specific group's beliefs or some institutional dogma, but that is because those beliefs and that dogma are themselves opposed to the wild, uncontrollable Spirit of God moving in the world today, just as they were opposed to the Spirit's mysterious movements in biblical times.

However, if heresy means denying what the Bible teaches us about God, Jesus, the Holy Spirit, love, grace, sin, forgiveness, judgment, and how to treat one another, then a heretic I most certainly am *not*. As

---

1. Also known as Saint Willie (for more on that, see my first book *Elvis, Willie, Jesus & Me*).

2. It's almost always a good time to listen to "My Heroes Have Always Been Cowboys"; now, however, is not . . . you're almost finished with the book!

you've read in these musings and sermons, it is *because* of my Christian faith and *because* of our Holy Bible that I affirm, include, and celebrate my LGBTQ sisters and brothers.

Therefore, I leave you with this slightly paraphrased truth from the Apostle Paul (Rom 8:38-39): For I am absolutely *convinced* that nothing . . . *nothing* . . . NUH - THING . . . not death, not life, not angels, not demons, not things present nor things to come, nor powers on earth, not even all the powers of hell itself, nor anything else in all of creation, can ever separate us from the love of God in Christ Jesus our Lord. And that certainly includes gender identity, sexual attraction, and loving relationships! To say otherwise is blasphemy.

And there you have it: the real heresy here is homophobia.

Resources:
Some Places to Start

Here are a few resources I continue to find very helpful and often share with others who are interested in learning more about LGBTQ inclusion and our Christian faith.

Websites

The Association of Welcoming and Affirming Baptists (AWAB)—awab.org
AWAB supports Baptist churches in being and becoming Welcoming and Affirming of all people regardless of gender identity or sexual orientation.

Believe Out Loud—believeoutloud.com
Believe Out Loud is an online community that empowers Christians to work for justice for lesbian, gay, bisexual, transgender, queer, intersex, and asexual (LGBTQIA) people.

Inside Out Faith—insideoutfaith.org
Founded by singer/songwriter Jennifer Knapp, the Inside Out Faith Foundation strives to highlight positive voices coming from within spiritual communities seeking to support LGBTQ dignity, and has as its goal to shine a spotlight on the people and stories that celebrate the diversity of integrated faith and sexuality.

Institute for Welcoming Resources (IWR)—welcomingresources.org
IWR's mission is to create resources that support the unconditional welcome of people of all sexual orientations and gender identities and their families in the church home of their choice.

Reconciling Ministries Network (RMN)—rmnetwork.org
Within the United Methodist Church, RMN works for full equality in membership, ordination, and marriage for God's lesbian, gay, bisexual, and transgender children.

Books

This I Know: A Simple Biblical Defense for LGBTQ Christians by Jim Dant (Nurturing Faith)

Building a Bridge: How the Catholic Church and the LGBT Community Can Enter into a Relationship of Respect, Compassion, and Sensitivity by James Martin, SJ (HarperCollins)

Love, Then Listen: Sharing My Son's Journey toward His True Gender by Daphne Reiley (Nurturing Faith)

The Loyal Opposition: Struggling with the Church on Homosexuality edited by Tex Sample and Amy DeLong (Abingdon Press)

To the Tune of a Welcoming God: Lyrical Reflections on Sexuality, Spirituality, and the Wideness of God's Welcome by David R. Weiss (Langdon Street Press)

Acknowledgments

It takes a lot of patience and encouragement on the part of others for books to be written—at least it does for my books. Thankfully, these virtues overfloweth in my family. With this assemblage in particular, my wife, Jency, and younger son, Daniel, read, reread, re-reread, and occasionally heard these columns and sermons at various stages; this finished product you hold is far better and easier to read because of their incredible eyes for detail, their excellent editorial suggestions, and their occasional biting sarcasm.[1]

I am also grateful to everyone who calls University Baptist Church their faith community—their willingness to be outwardly focused by bearing witness to the wildly inclusive love of Jesus and the wide diversity of God's kingdom right here in Starkville, Mississippi, continues to inspire me and makes me grateful to serve as their pastor; to Greg Cravens—the nationally syndicated illustrator and cartoonist (and family friend) whose imagination and talent provided yet another lively book cover; to Seth Oppenheimer—my friend, fellow justice-oriented clergy member, and the local rabbi, without whom there'd have been no rabbi with this preacher at the Pride parade (and yes, that's the real Rabbi Seth on the cover next to me); to all my friends at Smyth & Helwys Publishing and to Keith Gammons and Leslie Andres—my publisher and editor, respectively, who insist on making something not so bad into something really good. And thank YOU—you who continue to read my columns in the papers and online, who

---

1. The latter primarily from Daniel, but don't let Jency's sweet disposition fool you—she occasionally bites hard with sarcastic wit, too (and I love her all the more for it).

continue to listen to my sermons, and who continue to find my books meaningful.

About the Author

Since 2008, the good folks at the University Baptist Church of Starkville, Mississippi, have referred to Bert Montgomery as their pastor. For almost as long, students taking certain sociology and religion classes at Mississippi State University have called him their teacher. He studied at Mississippi State University, Union University, the Southern Baptist Theological Seminary, Mississippi College, Memphis Theological Seminary, and the Baptist Seminary of Kentucky, and he hung around long enough at three of those schools to actually get degrees. This is his fifth book.

For those who are curious about the author's music playlists, Bert's soundtrack while writing and assembling this book was mostly the discographies of the Indigo Girls, Jennifer Knapp, Queen, Cyndi Lauper, Lady Gaga, and, of course, Judas Priest.[1] You can contact Bert through his website, bertmontgomery.com.

---

1. It should go without saying (but I will say it anyway) that Elvis and Willie *occasionally* found their way into the mix, too. Willie, for the record (pun absolutely intended), sings two specific songs directly related to the themes in this book; your assignment is to go find them.